Ahoy! Quarterdeck!*
(with Sea Shanties supplement)

written and illustrated by

Harley L. Sachs

*Previously published as *Irma Quarterdeck Reports*

Harley L. Sachs

ISBN-10 1939381142
ISBN-13: 978-1-939381-14-9

Dedication

For Ulla Deborah Sachs, my best friend, wife, and most perceptive, objective and constructive critic.

Acknowledgements

Thanks to Lenny Rozansky, army cook and ashram leader who gave me my first sailing lesson, Sven Huldt who tried to shake me overboard, Richard Ziff who bought my first magazine article, Monk Farnham, editor of *Boating*, and Julius M. Wilensky, who remembered my boating articles and published the first edition of *Irma Quarterdeck Reports*.

Harley L. Sachs

Author's note from the first edition

No author writes in a vacuum. We are variously inspired by the world we live in. What we create is a fusion of often unrelated stimuli. The spark for Irma Quarterdeck began with the old Alka Selzer commercial, the dyspeptic husband sitting on the bed saying, "I can't believe I ate the whole thing." His wife answered, "You did it, Ralph. You ate it." Erma Bombeck's writing gave me a voice for columns by a sailing wife Irma Quarterdeck. So we have Ralph saying, "I can't believe I lost the anchor," and Irma's reply, "You did it, Ralph, you lost it."

Ralph and Irma Quarterdeck are a funny, loving couple who forgive one another's weaknesses and foolishness, but are not above teasing and kidding each other. They are confident of each other and secure in their marriage. Irma doesn't mind Ralph ogling the girls-- "Steady, Ralph, you'll fall overboard"-- because she notices "that cute college boy with the terrific shoulders" at Midas Marine. They are nice people to know.

Imaginary characters take on a life of their own. Writing each episode about Irma and Ralph was like visiting old friends. On his deathbed Balzac is said to have called for the doctor he created in *The Human Comedy*. Dickens went into deep depression after the death of Little Nell n *Oliver Twist*. Irma's terror when Ralph goes overboard brought tears to my eyes, yet they are all products of the imagination.

For Wescott Cove publishing company *Irma Quarterdeck Reports* also had to be full of useful boating information. Each episode is an example of education by anecdote, a teaching technique that is loved by some students and scorned by some faculty. Julius Wilensky and I both hoped that, besides being entertained by Irma and Ralph, readers will learn something useful.

Women too often let themselves be relegated to sexist "First Mate" status on boats. Irma Quarterdeck refuses to be merely a line handler and cook. Irma knows Ralph makes mistakes. She loves him and the life they have together too much to leave all the responsibility in his sometimes bumbling hands. Husbands do get lost, seasick, and even fall overboard. My hope is that Irma assertiveness will inspire other women to learn all they can about boating.

Books by Harley L. Sachs:

Novels

Queer Company
Never Trust a Talking Horse
The Gold Chromosome
Murder by Mail (Scratch—out!)!
Ben Zakkai's Coffin
The Search for Jesse Bram
The Mystery Club Solves a Murder
The Mystery Club and the Dead Doctor
The Mystery Club and the Hidden Witness
The Mystery Club and the Serial Widow
Conspiracy!
Murder in the Keweenaw
The Lollipop Murder
Betrayal
Retribution
Burnt Out
White Slave
Sam in Love
StopRape.com
The Accidental Courier

Collections of short fiction

Ahoy! Quarterdeck! (Irma Quarterdeck Reports)
Anna-Lena's Troll and other stories
Threads of the Covenant: The Jews of Red Jacket
Misplaced Persons

Non-Fiction

Freelance Non-Fiction Articles
The Misadventures of Cpl. Sachs
The 1957 Sachs Arctic Expedition
From Tent to Castle: Memoir of a Year-Long Honeymoon
IS
Chilly-Chilly BANG! How We Freelanced Through Europe's Coldest Winter in a VW with a Kid
Essays and Columns: 1992-2011
The Writing Life

Cartoons

Hunting the Mail Buoy and other hazards to navigation

Chapter 1

GETTING THE BOATING BUG

Our marriage was normal until Ralph got the boating bug. Other wives must know the feeling. Shopping trips were mysteriously re-routed to take a long, slow pass by the marina. Vacation plans always included a boat show. While I went shopping for a skirt to match the blouse I'd picked up on sale, Ralph would fill a plastic shopping bag with brochures for thirty footers, radar, GPS, depth sounders, and assorted boating gear modeled by cute things whose bikinis violated some city ordinance. It didn't stop there.

Subscriptions followed: to *Boater's Friend, Boatswain, Blue Water Boater, Yachtsperson,* and *Boatlubber*. The magazines piled up on the coffee table, burying our *National Geographics*. I knew we were in trouble when Ralph cancelled the subscription to *Playboy*!

Book clubs followed. One book club wasn't enough. Soon we were getting books every month. The Notice to Mariners was posted beside the john instead of *Reader's Digest*. Instead of "Life in These United States," I was rocking to "missing buoys" and "dredging operations at Sludge Harbor."

Ralph started clipping the ads that said "free catalog." We were already on a dozen mailing lists. There was Goldstein's Marine--a catalog every two months (whoever heard of a mariner named Goldstein?)-- Midwest Marine Supplies-- since when did we need a mile of half inch chain or a brass binnacle for the dining room? or a nude figurehead to breast the waters of our basement bar? I was going to put those genuine antique capstan bars to good use-- on Ralph's head!

But the magazines, books, and catalogues weren't enough. Ralph started buying stuff: belt buckles, for instance. He's got six: anchor, sailboat, ship's wheel, whale, dolphin, and an outboard motor buckle with a little propeller that actually turns. He wore it when we went dancing and it snagged my knit dress during a tango. I unraveled it down to a bare midriff before I realized why everyone was applauding!

He brought a Greek captain's hat with a Baltic badge--very international. He wears it to bed.

I caught Ralph one day in the shower trying out his foul weather gear. "Isn't it a little hard," I shouted, "trying to soap your armpits?"

He got a book on marlinespike seamanship, a set of fids, and a half mile spool of manila. He made rope mats for the kitchen, rope trivets, and place mats for the dining room. He put fancy rope work on the bed posts. He made a Turk's head bell lanyard and had to buy a bell to tie it to. That's on the headboard. "If you want anything, mate," he said to me with a leer, "just ring my bell."

"Not until you get those snippings of hemp off the sheets, you dingaling!"

Last month Ralph started reading Chapman, Bowditch, and Dutton-- all at once, and acquired a salty vocabulary. He rousts me out in the morning with "all hands on deck!" He got one of those whistles and pipes me to breakfast. I thought I take advantage of his seamanlike zeal and ordered him to "swab the galley deck" until I caught him about to sluice it down with five gallons of soapy water. There's no bilge in our basement bar. A busty figurehead, yes, but no bilge pump.

Guess what I got for Christmas? A sweatshirt stenciled "First Mate" and a bumper sticker that says "Boaters do it on the water." The shirt's pretty cute. I bought one of those canvas sun hats with brass grommets and a roped hem. Salty. Goldstein's Marine had a sale.

I've finally made a decision. After all those subscriptions, after getting tangled in the middle of the night with scratchy, unfinished rope work projects in bed, after listening to all those statistics about horsepower and outboard maintenance, I've got to put an end to it. There's an in the water boat show next week and I know just the thing to straighten out Ralph-- a sweet, salty runabout with one of those "cuddly" cabins. I'll model it myself in my new stowaway bikini. We're going to buy a boat.

Chapter 2

RALPH AND THE OUTBOARD THIEVES

Ralph turned paranoid when someone stole the outboard motor. Our boat trailer was turned with the hitch toward the garage to discourage someone from simply backing up, hitching the trailer on and driving it away. There was even an extra cable lock on one of the trailer wheels, but that wasn't enough. When we came home from a Saturday evening movie, there it was-- or rather, there it wasn't. Our 9.9 horsepower trolling motor was gone.

Ralph was pretty glum. "Bolt cutters," he groaned, picking up the nipped off shank of the padlock that had held the motor on the transom.

"Sure, Ralph," I said. "You've got a pair of $20 cheapie bolt cutters yourself. Remember how easy it was for you to cut the chain for my ten speed bike in front of the Hudson Bay Company when I lost the key?"

"Yeh, and I remember how you just sat in the car and laughed when the store security man showed up with the cops."

"I came to your rescue eventually didn't I?"

"It was still pretty embarrassing." Ralph looked at the neighboring houses. "Where are the witnesses when you really need some?"

Our couch potato neighbors, Ted and Gladys, said they hadn't seen anything. They'd been watching "Debbie Does Dallas" and some other XXX rated rental movie behind closed drapes. What goes on in the neighborhood doesn't interest them much.

We did the whole routine-- called the police, who came out, took down the details, and even made a perfunctory attempt to take fingerprints, but we knew we wouldn't see our outboard again.

It was pretty late by the time the police left, but Ralph called our insurance agent, waking him up. Because we have a small boat that has-- or had-- a motor under 25 horsepower we're covered by our home owner's policy. Yes, we had given the insurance company the serial number and were covered. How old was the motor? Five years. And what did we pay for it? A thousand dollars. Did we have the bill of sale to prove the purchase price? "Bill of sale?" Ralph choked. "Are you kidding? We bought it five years ago. I suppose if my kid were kidnapped you'd want proof of birth."

The insurance agent told Ralph we weren't insured against kidnappers, and what was the child's name?

"Ralph," I interrupted, "I have the bill of sale. It's filed with all the warranties." I keep complete files, a holdover from the days when I was a secretary.

Ralph gave me his grateful puppy look. "Yes, we have the bill of sale. No, we didn't sell our kid. It's the outboard motor that's stolen." He held his hand over the receiver. "Jesus! Is this guy stupid."

"You woke him up, Ralph."

Ralph listened to the agent and protested. "What? Is that all?" He turned to me. "We've been robbed again, Irma."

"What do you mean, Ralph?"

"The estimated life of an outboard is ten years, so the insurance company is depreciating our five year old motor to 50%. Then there's a $250 deductible on the home owner's policy. "We're only going to get $250 for the stolen motor."

"I knew we should have bought a separate marine policy."

Ralph pleaded with the insurance agent. "How about your just replacing the stolen motor instead of paying us cash?"

Even across the room I could hear the agent's laughter on the phone. Did Ralph expect the insurance agent to check out used motor dealers, garage sales, and flea markets? How much service did we expect for our $400 annual premium?

When we went shopping for another motor Ralph got sticker shock. In the five years our old motor was depreciating, inflation had driven up the price of new ones. Even with the measly $250 insurance payment, we'd have to kick in nearly two grand for a new motor. For a family that lives two paychecks short of bankruptcy, the theft really hurt. I could see another credit union loan and payments ahead.

Whatever we did to replace the stolen motor, we'd have to find out a better way to protect our investment than a padlock that could be snipped off by a $20 pair of bolt cutters.

We did a lot of shopping for another motor. Ralph would have settled for a used one, but I told him it was better to have a warranty and a projected availability of spare parts than to buy a used orphan that might have been abused in its youth and misbehave when we needed it most. When you're caught in a sudden storm you don't want your life to depend on a motor of dubious ancestry or condition.

We had to make the decision of two cycle or four cycle. I remembered the sheen of oil the old motor left on the water. I told Ralph that because two cycle engines are big polluters and are being phased out, we'd better get a four cycle. They're heavier, but are friendly to the environment.

We finally settled for a brand name we were confident wouldn't be outlawed by the EPA for polluting the waters.

We didn't only buy the motor. We also got a special lock bolt cutters wouldn't snip in thirty seconds. Why protect an investment of almost two thousand dollars with a $3 lock? Ralph also decided to bolt it to the transom.

"It sure looks nice," he said stepping back proudly and wiping his hands on his jeans.

I looked over my shoulder, up and down the street. The blinds were still drawn at Ted and Gladys's house. "It looks too nice," I commented. "As for bolts and a lock, Ralph, I don't think that's enough. Someone who really wants our motor will cut it out of the transom and wreck the boat into the bargain."

Ralph was crestfallen. "What'll we do, Irma? If this one's stolen we can't afford another."

I thought about it. "Look, Ralph-- we didn't buy this motor to show it off to the neighbors, did we?"

"Nope. We're going fishing."

"Right. We don't need to advertise this as a new motor. We have to make this motor not just hard to steal, but impossible to sell at some flea market."

"How do we do that?"

"Just wait." I went down in the basement and cut a piece of old inner tube from my ten speed. I cut a strip of steel flashing and dug out a big hose clamp, a roll of duct tape, and a screwdriver.

"Watch this," I said.

Ralph stood back in the driveway, puzzled.

I found the section of the motor column with the screw cap where the lower unit is serviced with lubricant. Careful not to cover the water intake or exhaust, I wrapped the column first with the inner tube, then with the piece of metal. I held it on securely with the hose clamp.

"It'll rust," Ralph said.

"Good. It's supposed to look like hell."

"Gee," Ralph said. "It looks like we've lost the filler screw, or maybe that there's a crack in the column."

"That's the way it looks, Ralph."

I took the motor cover off and wrapped a patch of duct tape around the fuel line. Then I took the nice, new "sold" tag and wrote on it with laundry marker, "Defective Lower Unit. Sold for parts."

"We could take the propeller off," I told Ralph, "but you'd probably try to re-use the old cotter pin and spin the prop off the first time you put the motor in reverse. I've a better idea."

I took off the motor cover and engraved the flywheel with our name, Ralph's driver's license number, and the date we purchased the motor. Then I stuck an "Operation Identification Crime Watch" sticker on the boat's transom. I carried the screwdriver and motor cover into the house.

Ralph was puzzled. "What are you doing, Irma?"

"You'll see." I brought out a couple of heavy, transparent plastic bags and taped them over the exposed outboard so everyone could see the patch on the gas line.

"It looks terrible," Ralph said.

It did. The new outboard looked like a piece of junk: no engine cover, a crummy patch on the column, and tape on the gas line to the carburetor. "Keep the motor cover locked in the house with our tackle boxes and the gas can, Ralph. Nobody's going to want to steal that outboard now."

Ralph gave me a big hug. He's so sexy.

"And another thing. We're getting a marine policy that pays us the replacement cost and no deductible."

There was a tear in Ralph's eye. He's so sentimental. "What would I do without you?"

"You big oaf. You'd have to row while I troll."

Chapter 3
RALPH AND THE SIGNAL FLAGS

"I think we need a mast for our boat," Ralph announced one night last October. He was lying in bed wearing his blue pajamas with the Save the Whale design and his Greek fisherman's cap with the Baltic insignia.

"A mast? On a car-topper? Are you going to hang yourself from the yardarm?"

"I was reading in Chapman that a grounded mast gives you 120 degrees of lightning protection. Think, Irma, if we were out on the water and lightning struck."

"If lighting were going to strike we'd have no business being out in the boat."

"Not only that," he went on, not listening as usual, "but if we had a mast, with a yardarm like you suggest, we could hoist flags."

I had seen the ads in the Goldstein Marine Supply sales catalog for novelty flags--pirate skull and crossbones, cocktail flags, B.Y.O.B. flags, mother-in-law flags, caught-a-marlin flags, sleeping bunny rabbits, and even one with interlocking male and female sex symbols meaning "do not disturb." "Do you plan to take up piracy?"

"Not that. None of that junk. Serious flags. Real flags." Then he reached under the mattress and pulled out an official-looking book bound in black. It looked like a secret code book you see in the movies, the kind the beautiful woman seduces the diplomat for. The fine print on the cover said it was published by the Defense Mapping Agency.

"Ralph! Where did you get that?"

"I ordered it from the government printing office. It's publication 102, the International Code of Signals. It tells you what all those pretty colored flags are for."

"I thought they were for parades."

"No, they're for real. They go back a long way, very historical. There's an international agreement for flag communication."

"That's what radios are for, Ralph. Let's go to sleep."

He turned out the light but he wasn't finished. "What if we drifted offshore and met a Cuban gunboat? We don't have a radio. I don't speak Spanish."

"Ralph, it's an aluminum car topper without even a mast. We don't go out in the ocean. We're not going to meet any Cuban gunboats."

Ralph's voice from under the covers was worried and determined. "We need a set of signal flags."

"They cost over a hundred bucks!" I said.

"That's a lot." That stopped him. If there's one thing we didn't have to buy it was signal flags. I went to sleep convinced he'd forget all about it.

He didn't. He studied that book. And he laughed, but he wouldn't tell me what he was laughing about. I figured I'd find out for myself when he left for work, but either he hid the book, or took it with him. I couldn't find it. On Saturday when we went to the mall, I caught him coming out of the yard goods store with a package. Sure enough. He had bought a quantity of yellow, red, blue, black, and white cloth, some strong seam tape, and polyester thread.

"I'm not going to sew you a set of signal flags," I said.

"Of course not. I'm going to sew them myself."

And he did. I couldn't believe it. Ralph wouldn't sew a button on his shirt, but there he was with the sewing machine, struggling with the bobbin, threading the needle, cutting fabric. Soon the floor of the TV room was full of snippings of thread and bits of cloth. Night after night instead of watching his usual sitcom, Ralph sewed flags. Finally, around Christmas, he was done. He had the whole alphabet, ten numeral pennants, and even three repeaters. Thirty-nine flags, all different.

"While you're at it," I asked one night during a commercial, "why not fix the pocket on my apron? It's torn."

"Sure," he said, without looking up from the signal book. I caught him looking at me and snickering.

He fixed the apron and at Christmas there was a package with a tag, "For the nauti-gal cook." It was an apron made like the signal flags: a blue one with a white X on it, a flag with red white and blue vertical stripes, and a blue horizontal flag with yellow above and below. It was finished off by two numeral pennants, the blue one with a white spot and the white one with a red cross. Ralph had neatly sewn a nice pocket without disturbing the pattern. After thirty-nine flags, he had to have learned something about sewing. "Kind of garish, isn't it?"

Ralph smiled. "Looks good on you."

"What's it mean?"

Ralph was tight lipped. "Private joke."

"Alright, Ralph, hand it over. The code book."

For the first time I got to peek inside. He had shown me the colored end papers, but not the clever arrangement and classification of the signals. The apron was made of the designs for MTD28. In the alphabetical listing I found that all the M's were medical, that MTD meant to administer a medicine, and number 28 was Compressi Magnesii Trisilicas--stomach medicine. "Very funny, Ralph."

"It's our secret. Would you prefer the code for patient is pregnant'?"

"Not again, Ralph. I should make one for you." I leafed in the code of signals. "How about, Patient has delirium tremens'? You can wear it when you tend bar under that half naked female figurehead you got from Goldstein's Marine."

"Love it! What a conversation piece. You can send all kinds of signals with these flags. You don't need to know Chinese or Russian or Spanish. It's all in the book. Man overboard, I am disabled, I am dragging my anchor.' And you don't need batteries to send them."

"You need one more, Ralph. The big orange one with a black square and circle."

"The international distress flag. Right! Tomorrow night."

I glad to say we haven't needed those signal flags to communicate with Cuban gun boats. We don't have a radio, but we did stick on a mast and got the prize the next Fourth of July for being the smallest "dressed" vessel in the Venetian parade. And when the outboard died that international distress flag brought someone to our rescue. We've had a lot of fun with those flags, and as a bonus, Ralph learned to sew-- pockets, buttons, zippers, and one of those "do not disturb" flags that he hoists on a lanyard over the bed.

Chapter 4

RALPH AT THE RAMP

Did I tell you Ralph got a sailing dinghy? He picked it up for almost nothing from somebody's back yard. He fixed it and carries it on top of the camper like a security blanket. That husband of mine can't be without a boat. He says he's a descendent of Noah. "Got to be prepared if it floods again," he says, rolls his eyes, and touches his Greek fisherman's hat for assurance.

When we drove west on vacation, the dinghy had to come along. At Yellowstone he got blown off the lake. When we got to Portland, Oregon he would have launched in the Columbia River but one look at those waves whipped up by wind and tide and he let me talk him into Portland's other river, the Willamette.

Willamette Park near John's Landing has a ramp wide enough to launch six boats at a time. "Oh, wow!" Ralph said. "I can hardly wait."

"Wait, Ralph. Let's watch for awhile first." We sat on the bank and watched as a husband, eager as Ralph, backed his car and boat trailer down the paved ramp for one of those snap launches. You know, slam on the brakes and the boat flies off into the water. The wife was in the boat with a mooring line in her hand. The launch was perfect. The boat scooted onto the river.

The husband jumped out of the car and ran along the dock. "Throw me the line!"

She threw it-- and he caught the end, but it wasn't attached to a cleat. The current was carrying boat and wife past the end of the dock. The husband tripped as the loose end of the line he was running with caught on the dock. Luckily, a bystander with a long reach caught the woman's hand... both almost fell in. In the meantime, the car was slowly slipping down the ramp into the river. Pandemonium.

"You wouldn't see me do that," Ralph said.

Another runabout had been launched just as we arrived and six fat people, looking like eight, crowded into it. They headed upstream through the shallows, pretty close to some big rocks. "Look!" Ralph exclaimed. "They've hit something!"

The boat lurched, heaved up on one side, and everyone fought for their balance, but they did not stop. They gunned the motor instead. Like a car driver lurching out of a chuckhole, they crunched over a boulder. "They'll break a prop!" Ralph laughed. "Look, now they're checking to see if they've sprung a leak. Nope. There they go."

"They're probably out looking for an accident," I said as the runabout disappeared upstream.

My voice was drowned out by the roar of a gleaming jet boat with twin chromium phallic exhaust pipes thrusting out the back. Vroom. The driver was a macho man with a cowboy hat. In the bow one of those svelte dark-haired beauties was posing in a minimal bikini for maximum effect. "Boy!" Ralph said.

"You're drooling, Ralph."

"Some life, huh?"

"She won't wear that outfit when she gets stretch marks," I said. The jet boat suddenly slowed. The cowboy hat had blown off. Macho man turned the jet to retrieve it.

"Help me with the dinghy," Ralph said.

"You'll never catch them, Ralph."

"Gotta have my boat. What's a boat for? Let's launch."

I helped him get it down off the camper. When he has to carry out the garbage or bring in the groceries, Ralph has a bad back, but when he's launching that dinghy, or carrying the outboard you wouldn't believe he'd ever been in traction.

We got the dinghy down but I refused to get in. Instead I watched as a couple of those water scooters roared in circles on the river, zipping around the sailboats from the Willamette sailing club, jumping the jet boat wakes, and terrorizing canoeists. Into the midst of that madness rowed Ralph. He has a sail for that dinghy, and when he got out on the river he put it up, sat back, and waited. No wind.

The jet boat with the macho man, now without his hat, came by like an express train. The nearly naked female with her fixed, disdainful smile never noticed Ralph. He just sat there like a miner in a tin bathtub on Saturday night who got in without the soap.

Then, like Hell's Angels on the water, the two clowns on the jet skis whipped past a kid on a sailboard, dumping him with their wake, and headed for Ralph. "Ralph, look out!"

You never saw that sail come down so fast. Ralph picked up the oars and rowed madly for the ramp. I didn't say I told you so, he was so crestfallen already. We loaded the dinghy on the camper and took our places again on the bank.

We didn't have long to wait. A paunchy, middle aged man in 1950's Bermuda shorts, love beads, and carrying an open can of beer launched a hand-me-down runabout loaded with his little boy, a picnic basket, and a day's supply of brew. Everything went smoothly until they started the motor and got out on the river. Then there was shouting and excitement. They had forgotten the drain plug.

As fast as they could, they headed back for the ramp. The man in Bermudas ran for the car, backed down the trailer, hooked up the winch rope to the bow of the boat, and cranked madly. It was too late.

While Ralph and I watched the stern of the runabout went under. The boy stood petrified as the water rose around him. The picnic cooler floated off downstream accompanied by a few empty beer or pop cans. Ralph shook his head. "Some people just shouldn't be on the river."

"I'm glad you brought the dinghy," I said. "I haven't had this much entertainment in years. Just don't launch it again without first checking the waters."

Chapter 5

IRMA'S DUFFEL BAG

Ralph always makes fun of my purse. Every time I grope for the car keys he pulls his out of his pocket and gives me that irritating look of male superiority. "Those women's purses," he says, and shakes his head.

"Women's clothes don't have pockets like you do. Your slacks have four pockets and your sport shirt two more. I should know. I'm always emptying them when I do the laundry. this sun dress has just enough material to hold me."

"Yeh," he says, and rolls his eyes.

"Women need more stuff. So I carry a purse." You'd be surprised what I carry in mine. Besides the usual essentials, I've got a little flashlight, a pocket knife, and a note pad.

When he goes to the beach, all he has is his trunks, a pair of flip flops and a towel, but I take a folding chair, umbrella, sunscreen, something to read, a snack that he ends up eating, sunglasses, a wide-brimmed hat, lipstick, a mirror, and a few other essentials. I let him carry it.

When we go fishing, it's much the same. Ralph's idea of loading up the aluminum boat is to throw in the fishing tackle, gas can, bait, and a cooler of Moosehead beer. But I have my boating duffel. Ralph still doesn't know exactly what's in it. That's my secret.

It all started last summer. We were out drowning worms one Sunday afternoon, one of those hot days when the fish don't bite. We were passed by an old man and a couple of kids, his grandchildren, in a wooden skiff powered by a noisy, air cooled outboard with no motor cover. It sounded more like a chain saw than a fishing outboard. The motor quit and the man yanked on the starter cord a dozen times, fiddled with the thing, and finally got it going again.

I forgot about them until I saw that the sky was getting dark. Thunderheads were rolling in. "Time to go, Ralph," I said.

It's frightening how quickly conditions can change on the water. One minute you're in paradise. The next you're fighting for your life. There's only a thin sheet of aluminum between you and deep water. Sitting on a cushion inside the boat is very different from being up to your neck in cold water if the boat sinks out from under you. We hardly had his silly cement can anchor up before the wind started to blow.

The rain started in big drops like teacups, soaking us instantly. As we rounded a point, there was the old man and his grandchildren. They were crying and he was yanking at that old outboard. This time it wouldn't go. He had hurt his hand and couldn't use his oars. They were in real trouble.

We pulled alongside. "We'll give you a tow," I shouted. Can you believe, between us and that skiff there wasn't a decent piece of line? The old man had an old cow tail of manila just long enough to tie the boat to a post. We didn't even have that, since our boat stays on the trailer. We just had Ralph's clothes line anchor rope. Ridiculous.

We ended up side by side, which wasn't such a bad idea, because boats tied together alongside are easier to steer than if one is swinging from side to side behind the other.

The old man could hold onto our boat with only one hand. "Cut my hand on the motor," he shouted, and held up what looked a lot worse than it turned out to be.

The granddaughter was about twelve, the grandson about eight. The boy was crying, but the girl gamely held on to our boat.

"Don't get your fingers mashed," I said, as the two boats jostled. I was surprised how quickly the waves could build up.

It wasn't far to shore and we pulled up on the beach to wait on the porch of someone's cottage until the shower quit. By that time there was plenty of water in the skiff, and no bailer except the can their bait was in.

We didn't have a first aid kit for the man's hand. The old man-- I forgot his name-- was despondent. "They'll never let me take the kids fishing again," he said. He had that fearful look of someone who is at the end of his competence. "My wife wants me to get rid of the boat and motor and move to a condo in Florida."

"What's the matter with the motor, anyway?" Ralph asked.

"Dirty plug, maybe. Or sediment in the carburetor," the man said. "I was so excited about taking the kids fishing, I left my tool kit in the car. Can I use yours?"

Ralph gulped. "Don't have one."

"Uh huh," I thought. I looked out at the lake. There were a couple of fishing boats still out and some kids screaming along on a Hobicat, oblivious to the rain.

Ralph went down to the boats and started bailing them out.

"What tools do you carry?"

The old man thought a moment. "Screw driver, pliers, some wire and electrical tape, bit of gas line hose, clamps, spark plug wrench, and some spares."

"Wait a second." I dug out the little pad and pen I carry in my purse. "Start over. What spares?" I asked.

"Spark plugs, grease, and an impeller."

I wasn't sure what an impeller was, but I was going to find out.

He saw what I was writing down. "You could add a spare prop, nut, and cotter pins."

It made a long list. Later I watched while the old man, his cut hand wrapped in a handkerchief, instructed Ralph in the removal of the fuel filter. It was clogged.

"Probably rust in the bottom of that old gas can," he said.

Ralph cleaned the filter.

"Let me put it back on," I said. "It doesn't hurt for a woman to be able to do these things." It wasn't difficult.

"Tell your Mom that your grandpa's pretty smart," I told the granddaughter. "And get him to teach you how to run the outboard. You're old enough."

"The fish will be biting now," Ralph said.

The old man and the grandchildren left and we fished awhile longer. Ralph caught a small mouth bass.

When I we got home I took out my list. I found the owner's manual to the outboard and located the impeller on one of the exploded view drawings. It's nothing but a little, rubber thing that pumps the water so the engine won't overheat. But if a plastic bag or something else clogs the water intake, the impeller can be damaged.

I picked up an impeller for our make and model outboard and threw together a few other items. Instead of ordinary pliers I put in one of those cute vice grips that give you a free hand, plus a significant first aid kit, not just a couple of plastic strip bandages. I added a couple of plastic, emergency raincoats we picked up at some bank grand opening. It made a significant pile of gear.

I dug out Ralph's old army duffel bag from the basement. I realized that it would be impossible to find a spark plug on the bottom of a duffel bag, so I resurrected one of my old leather purses and marked it "Tools" with a laundry pen. A purse is a perfect tool case-- lots of compartments for small things like pocket wipes to clean the grease off your hands.

Now when we go boating we don't need a checklist. Just grab the duffel.

"What have you got in there?" Ralph asked when he saw it. "The overflow from your purse?"

"That's my boating duffel. The life jackets go on top so we can put them on when we get in the boat. But there's other stuff." I opened up the bag and took out one item. "A hundred feet of nylon line," I said. "Just in case you have to tow someone. Here's the flare kit the Coast Guard requires."

"Good idea, Irma. You think of everything. What else have you got in there? Any snacks?"

I closed the duffel. "A woman's got to have her secrets." I didn't want to tell him how much I spent for a spare propeller. If he hits a rock he'll be glad I bought it. There's no guarantee there'll be someone out there to rescue us when it's our turn to get in trouble on the water.

Chapter 6

A BOAT BY ANY OTHER NAME...

"What are we going to name our boat?" I asked Ralph as we poked around the yard. All around us people were getting their boats ready to launch. Canvas covers were off, and we could see all those names.

"That should be easy," Ralph said. "It took us only about fifteen minutes to name our kids when they came along."

Funny, isn't it? Fifteen minutes to pick a name for your child, a name he or she will carry their entire life. A name becomes the person, and vice versa. It's a serious business, like a karma. Your fate is in your name.

For instance, people with the middle name of Wayne keep turning up on lists of murderers. I wouldn't name a child Wayne. And I wouldn't name a boy "Sue" unless I wanted him to grow up to be my son the lawyer.

In the back of my dictionary there must be more than a couple of hundred male and female names. Naming a child is easy. Naming a boat isn't. Just to show you how difficult naming a boat can be, somebody's published a book of ten thousand boat names!

Boat names have a prominent place in our vocabulary, and that makes naming a boat especially difficult. You can call a boat just about anything... or can you?

"A boat name isn't like a child's name," Ralph said. "A boat name reflects something of the personality of the owner, too. Look at that one!" He pointed at an expensive one-off hull designed to beat the racing rules. "There's a name I definitely wouldn't use: 'Blow Job.'"

I agreed. "A boat name shouldn't suggest something risqué' about the owner. Look at the trouble the cruiser 'Monkey Business' caused Gary Hart."

"He could have called it 'Sin King,'" Ralph said, waggishly.

"Sure, Ralph. I can just hear him calling the coast guard on the radio. 'This is Sin King.' And the coast guard's reply, 'You're sinking? What's your position?'"

"What about calling your boat 'Nuclear Submarine'? Then when you got on the radio you could say, 'This is Nuclear Submarine'. Or you could name it 'Smuggler' or 'Snort" or 'Quick Fix.'"

"Ralph, that'd be looking for trouble from the drug enforcement agency. You'd be boarded every five minutes."

"If you wanted respect from the authorities, you could call your boat 'Commanding Officer' or 'Fleet Commander' or maybe 'The Admiral.'" He put on his authoritative voice. "This is 'The Admiral' calling. Bring me out a can of gas immediately."

I shook my head. "There really are forbidden names, like 'May Day'. If you called your boat 'May Day' every time you got on the radio you'd bring out the rescue squad."

Ralph was thoughtful. "The name has to be something understandable even in a poor radio transmission. And not too long. It shouldn't be too expensive, either. If you order fancy boat name decals you pay by the letter. A one letter name would be cheapest."

"What would be a one letter name? A single digit number?"

Ralph smiled. "You could call it '1.'"

"When you got your second boat would it be '2,' or '1 II'? No, Ralph."

"A nuclear physicist might call his boat 'U235.' That'd be cheap. Only four letters."

"Someone on the radio would think it was a German submarine."

"I guess that's out," Ralph admitted. "My German accent isn't convincing. Besides, I'm not a nuclear physicist."

We were stumped. Ralph reminded me that submarines are named after fish, but who'd want to call their yacht 'Herring' or 'Squid'? Following his line of reasoning, I admit that 'Cod' would be cheap, only three letters to paint. 'Cod' just isn't, well, evocative enough. A pleasure boat's name has to express something happy. 'Barracuda,' 'Black Marlin,' or 'Swordfish' might do for some game fisherman, but not for us.

At the back of the boat yard was a little day sailor, much in need of paint. Someone had crudely lettered its transom 'Queen Mary.' It just wasn't appropriate. It's pretentious to name your boat after something really famous. Some boats have laid claim on the name for all time. Those names are, well, taboo.

I wouldn't name our boat 'Dorade,' for instance. Those rain and spray proof, self-draining ventilator boxes that you see on some yachts were first installed on 'Dorade' in the 1930's and the name stuck.

Ralph says those special boat names are retired, like a famous ball player's number. Ralph can name several sportsman's jersey numbers, but he's more of a baseball and football fan than I am.

You could make up a game of trivia based entirely on boat names. Other famous boat names are 'Gypsy Moth,' Chichester's circumnavigating yacht, which he named after the plane he tried to fly around the world. 'Gypsy Moth' is on display outside London beside another famous vessel, the clipper ship 'Cutty Sark.' You could name a whiskey after that one, but to call a yacht 'Cutty Sark' just wouldn't be right.

Ralph says it would sound like you named your boat after a whiskey, and suggested we call ours 'Moosehead' after his favorite beer. I nixed that one.

Joshua Slocum sailed his boat, 'Spray,' around the world. Some sailors have named their boats 'Spray' out of veneration or the ambition to sail in Slocum's wake. Then there was 'Tinkerbelle,' that tiny boat Manry sailed across the Atlantic. 'Jester' sailed in the first single-handed, trans-Atlantic race. And don't forget 'America's cup, or 'Bluenose.' There have been a whole series of 'Wanderers,' 'Pen Duick's, 'Columbia's, and 'Endeavor's.

Literature has given us boat names, too, like the 'Nautilus,' the submarine in Jules Verne's book. 'Dulcibella,' a converted lifeboat, figures in the 1903 thriller, *Riddle of the Sands*, and Melville's 'Rights of Man' in *Billy Budd*. Here's a trivia question: what was the name of the boat in the television series, Gilligan's Island? Guppy? Minnow?

History has given us boat names associated with explorers and colonists, like the 'Mayflower,' Henry Hudson's 'Half Moon,' and of course Christopher Columbus's 'Pinta,' 'Nina,' and 'Santa Maria.' Captain Cook's ship was the 'Resolution.' The Arctic was explored by the Norwegian 'Fram,' which Ralph says stands for "Forward!" Scott went to Antarctica on the 'Discovery.' And Darwin sailed on the 'Beadle,' a voyage that produced his *Origin of the Species*. Thor Heyerdahl had his 'Kon-Tiki,' but Ralph says he wouldn't name our boat after a raft.

Then there was the 'Bounty,' Captain Bligh's ship. To name your boat the 'Bounty' might encourage mutiny, or at least insubordination.

There are also famous warships. Drake sailed the 'Golden Hind.' Ralph says that suggests a tanned nudist. We remember the 'Constitution,' known as 'Old Ironsides,' the 'Monitor' and 'Merrimac' from the Civil War, and the battleship 'Maine' from the Spanish-American war. The Russians have their battleship 'Potemkin' and cruiser 'Aurora'; and the Germans the 'Bismarck' and the cruiser the 'Graf Spee.' But who'd want to name a yacht after a warship?

Some warship names like 'Implacable,' 'Invincible,' and 'Indomitable' are meant to intimidate the enemy. Ralph suggests Incorrigible. Too many letters.

Some boat names are unlucky. Who would want to call their boat 'Titanic'? Or 'Edmund Fitzgerald,' lost on Lake Superior? Or the 'Mary Celeste,' found mysteriously abandoned at sea? Or 'Exxon Valdez?' To name a yacht after one of those would be to court disaster.

Ralph disagrees."If you named your boat after a supertanker, when you're out in the fog people would give you plenty of room."

For several Sundays Ralph and I wandered the marinas and boat yards thinking about names. There were plenty with girl's names, like 'Suzy Q' or 'Madelyn.' I didn't want a female competitor for Ralph's affections.

"How about something out of astronomy or mythology?" Ralph suggested. "Like Vega or Polaris, Castor or Pollux for stars used in navigation. Neptune was the Roman god of the sea. And there's Poseidon. Wasn't he the Greek sea god?"

Yes, but in the movie the 'Poseidon' capsized. No thanks. Still, there are many Greek names that are lovely on boats--Ariadne, Phaedra. The 'Argo' was Jason's in his search for the Golden Fleece, giving us the nautical term Argonauts. Seems a bit much to name a mere pleasure boat after the Argonauts. What about Hydra or Hecate?

"Hecate?" Ralph says, "No way. That name's for staunch female feminists only. Even 'Lesbos' would be better than 'Hecate.'"

Kraken and Kelpie are both sea monsters, but could make nice boat names.

There are geographical boat names, like 'Finisterre,' a cape in northern Spain, and Cape Horn.

Ralph was getting desperate. "Why don't we just call it Boat? Four letters and be done with it."

I wasn't willing to settle for that. I remembered the names people use for their cottages, like Bide-a-Wee, or Escape, Happy Days, or Snug Harbor or The Anchorage. Some combine names, like HarMorChar, from Harley, Morton and Charles. A husband Marvin and his wife Louise named their yacht Marvelous, sort of an inside joke, abbreviating "Marvin'Lou's." A game inventor calls his boat

'Gamesman'ship,' but that's too cute. It also takes up too much room on the transom.

"You've given me an idea," Ralph said. "We'll name it after us. Like a rebus: 1/4DECK. Cheap. Not too many letters. Catchy, too."

I still wasn't satisfied. We had gone round and round. "Maybe the boat itself will suggest its name. Something in the character of the lines."

"You're right, Irma. Let's buy the boat first and name it afterwards. I have a feeling that it's easier to buy a boat than it is to name one."

Chapter 7

SHOPPING FOR A BOAT

All boats are a compromise. In fact, when Ralph and I shopped for ours I felt more compromised than a politician trying to satisfy voters of every possible persuasion, religion, sexual preference, and color. Ocean cruisers compromise speed for strength and the volume demanded to stow food, water, and fuel. To reduce windage, some boats have lush decks and no standing headroom below. Shoal draft for gunkholing means reduced performance on the wind. Fin keels and spade rudders respond quickly for maneuvers around racing courses, but don't track as well as long, traditional keel boats. Tall masts for light air demand stays and shrouds whose windage makes a boat more tender. We had to decide whether we'd pay a yard for storage or keep our boat in the back yard. Trailerable boats have to be light enough to pull and narrow enough to haul without a WIDE LOAD permit. But then they probably have no standing headroom. The compromises go on and on. And of course, there's the compromise between Ralph's dream boat and how much we could afford to invest. Deciding on those compromises was an education and almost an ordeal.

Besides all the boating supply catalogs from Goldstein's Marine and their ilk, Ralph loaded the headboard bookcase of our bed with annual boat show issues of *Boatswain, Blue Water Boater, Boater's Friend,* and *The Yachtsperson.* I tried to tell him that the manufacturers listed in the boat show issues were the ones that paid for the space as advertising. The best boat for us might be in the category, "None of the Above."

"Gee, you're right, Irma. I better send for some brochures." Ralph pulled the reader's service bingo cards out of all the magazines and marked the numbers. That put us on a couple of hundred junk mail lists. The postman was beginning to hate us. We were flooded with information about boats. When the brochures weren't free, Ralph would send the five dollars. There were even advertising videotapes to be borrowed that showed the boats in action. Instead of rental movies, we looked at advertising tapes.

All that by a guy who hates shopping. When I go to the mall Ralph would just as soon stay in the car like somebody's dog. When it comes to looking for a boat, that's a different story.

It seemed like everybody in the world was trying to sell us their boat, and we already had two-- that little dinghy and the aluminum fishing boat.

Ralph checked the classified ads in the newspaper and in the Boat US members' magazine.

"Here's a guy who wants to trade a condo for a yacht," Ralph said, "and someone else who wants to trade a yacht for a ranch in Oregon. I guess nobody's ever satisfied."

I agreed. "I read that the average boat owner keeps a boat only two or three years, then buys something bigger."

"If that's the case, there should be plenty of smaller, used boats we could pick from."

We had a good idea of how much we could afford to spend. What we were really doing with all this shopping was finding out how much boat we could reasonably expect to get for that money. New, ocean-going boats in the twenty to twenty-five foot range cost about a thousand dollars a foot, but there was a point about twenty-six or twenty-seven feet where stresses on a longer hull dictated a kind of exponential increase in strength, weight, and price. You could easily spend three thousand a foot or more. At around forty feet, well, change your name to Rockefeller and hope the bank takes the check: a hundred thousand or more. Just saying prices like that was like trying to talk after swallowing a mouthful of Mexican peppers.

"Look at it this way," Ralph said. "Under the current tax laws you can't deduct the interest on a car loan, but you can deduct interest on a boat as a second home. It just has to have bunks, a head, and a galley."

I pointed to an ad for a huge ketch, priced at over a hundred thousand, and appropriately named "Albatross." The Ancient Mariner would agree. "And interest payments substantially less than our combined salaries," I added. "We can't give up eating."

In spite of what we had invested in brochures, a new boat was out. What we bought had to be a compromise. It had to be used, not new, or we couldn't get anything but a day sailor.

Ralph said, "What we need is the boating equivalent of the car that was only driven to church on Sunday by a widow."

"You got it half right, Ralph. We could find a deal in an estate sale, or a foreclosure."

"Or a divorce," Ralph said with a wink. "Wife gets house and husband gets tired of living on the boat, sells it and moves aboard a condo."

The shopper in me was aroused. "It's time we put aside the magazines and brochures and got serious," I said. "Let's make some phone calls."

What resulted was fun and educational. Every used boat has a story to tell. There were dramas and heartbreaks. Manry had written how he had found Tinkerbelle in the back yard of an old couple who cried when he took the neglected boat away. Their early married life was in that boat. We talked to all kinds of owners. Some had moved up to bigger boats, and needed cash from the old one. Some had overblown expectations, expecting to get the price of a new boat out of a neglected hull.

Anyone looking for an older boat could do well scouting the back yards of neighborhoods. There are an unbelievable number of boats under tarps and languishing to be back in the water.

We looked at a magnificent, old sloop with long overhangs and a bowsprit. It was wooden, and exuded an aura of south sea adventures, coconuts, and bananas hanging in the forepeak. It also exhaled the smell of decay. Ralph lifted the engine cover. "Beware of freshly-painted bilges," he said and stuck his marlinespike into the wood of the engine mount. He shook his head like a doctor who opens a patient to find a fatal cancer. "Rot."

I almost asked him if he could fix it, but I remembered the shelf he put in the laundry room, the one that drops the detergent every time the washing machine does its dance. How could he replace an engine bed? Never.

Another wooden boat was so poorly maintained that you not only smelled decay in the forepeak, you could see light between the planks. We decided not to look at any wooden boats after that.

Fiberglass is so durable that every fiberglass boat ever made must still be seaworthy, or reasonably so. Let a wooden boat go and it'll soon rot out, but fiberglass lasts.

Fiberglass isn't fool proof. We checked out a Luger kit boat someone had built. It was cute and cozy, but when Ralph lay down on the ground under its trailer he said, "Look."

All along the keel were streaks where the water had run out of it. We have an old Luger kit boat brochure with pictures of the easy assembly in my file. "He didn't know how to lay up the fiberglass seam," Ralph said. "See where the water ran out? It must have sunk when they launched it." We decided against buying a used kit boat or any home-made.

But we also saw other flaws. A keel boat up in the yard on its cradle showed a crack where water had leaked out of the bilge. "A void in the hull," Ralph said. "Must have filled with water, frozen during winter lay-up, and cracked the fiberglass."

We were beginning to learn about boats.

If a used car breaks down on the highway, you can abandon it. If your boat breaks down, it may abandon you.

We visited yards within a hundred miles of our home. They were full of abandoned dreams, old motor boats with gaping seams, broken windows, torn canvas, and unpaid storage bills. We saw home-builts, like the fifty foot ferrocement hull that was never finished, the owner having run out of energy or money or both. There were bargains among them. We just missed buying a beautiful twenty-five footer the yard owner had taken possession of and would sell for the unpaid storage fees. "If we do buy a boat we'd better be careful who we store it with," Ralph said.

We found a reasonably-priced twenty-two foot sloop, an older model that had not been in the water for several years. We got as far as inspecting the sails, which had been stored in a barn. Field mice had nested in the sail bags, chewing the Dacron to tatters. I already knew the cost of replacing a suit of sails and had no confidence in Ralph's ability to sew them himself. Flags, maybe, not sails.

We finally found a 1973 Coronado 23. Narrow enough to trailer. It had a keel, but shouldn't be too heavy for our pick-up to pull. The owner, a military man, was being transferred to a missile base in Nebraska and the government wouldn't pay to move the boat. There wasn't any water deep enough in Nebraska to float it. The outboard motor was new. The sails were OK. No field mice, at least, and nothing torn or patched. The price was right. $4200. He would settle for $4000.

It took several phone calls to find an insurance company that would write a policy on a boat over ten years old.

Ralph was ready to write a check post-dated a few days so we could move money to the checking account, but I wanted a bona-fide bill of sale. I got the serial number off the boat and the registration number, and wrote up a bill of sale that listed everything he said was included, especially the outboard motor. I didn't want half the gear to disappear. Anchors and compasses were expensive. I didn't want to charge an unnecessary order at Goldstein's Marine. The bill of sale also stipulated that Captain so-and-so was the sole and legitimate owner of the boat, that there was no lien on it. Between the lines, that meant that the boat wasn't stolen.

When it came to signing the bill of sale, the officer hesitated. It turned out that he still owed the bank a thousand dollars on the boat. It wasn't really his.

After all that shopping and compromising, Ralph was disappointed.

"What's the name of the bank?" I asked. There was no deal until I got the lender to agree to the sale. Then they'd know that the boat was changing hands and they would get their money.

The bank agreed to the sale and the big moment came. The bill of sale was duly signed, the check handed over in exchange for the registration papers and title to the trailer.

"It looks like we own a boat," Ralph said.

I'm told there are two happy days in a boat owner's life: the day the boat is bought and the day it is sold. After all that shopping and compromising, we had a trailerable keel boat with sitting head room. It was an older model, but seaworthy. The price was right. We would arrange the insurance, get a license plate, and pick up the boat and trailer on Saturday.

Ralph was worried. As we pulled out of the Captain's driveway, he said, "We didn't get it surveyed," he said. "Maybe we should have had it surveyed. And we should have given it a test sail. I hope we haven't made a mistake."

"It's a compromise, Ralph," I said. "There wasn't time for everything."

"Maybe we should name it 'Compromise.'"

I could see he still wanted a twenty-seven footer, one that could cross oceans. "There you go again," I said, trying to imitate Reagan in his debate against Carter. "Those darn names. Compromise has too many letters, Ralph."

"Just so we don't call it 'Folly,'" Ralph said. We accelerated on the ramp and entered the stream of freeway traffic. He was quiet for awhile. "I know what we should call it. 'Dreamer.'"

"'Dreamer.' That's a nice name. Boats are what dreams are made of."

Chapter 8:

OUR TRAILER ADVENTURE

Laurel and Hardy, who our kids used to call "Fatty and Skinny," made a film once about a sailboat. In it the two comedians raise the sails while the boat is still on the trailer. As everyone expects, along comes a wind and chaos results. Ralph and I didn't raise the sails on 'Dreamer' when we first picked it up. Nor did we raise the mast and try to drive under freeway bridges, but the result was nearly as chaotic.

After years of hauling our aluminum fishing boat on its little trailer, we thought we knew what we were doing. But the Coronado 23, stripped, weighs 2200 pounds. Add the trailer to that, plus the outboard, two anchors, fuel tank, and sundry gear, and we had a load of over three thousand pounds. That may be more than Ralph's six cylinder pickup truck weighs.

Just to give his tired vehicle a chance, we had taken off the camper and left it beside the driveway. We have a two car garage, but with the aluminum boat in one half, the lawn mower and snow blower in the other, I had to park my Suburu in the driveway. We left the camper on its stilts slowly sinking into the lawn. The place looked like a parking lot. I could just see the local vigilantes from the "Keep our Neighborhood Neat" committee taking notes and cell phone photos of the mess.

Ralph was used to driving the pickup with the camper on it. When we bounced out of the neighborhood, he remarked, "Seems kind of light in the rear end." The truck did seem to kick up its heels.

The captain was waiting for us when we arrived at his house to pick up the boat and trailer. Well schooled in the art of moving at government expense, he had a trailer loaded, covered snugly with a tarp, and was ready to leave for Nebraska. As he explained, he would be paid commercial rates for whatever he was able to move himself, and make a few bucks on the deal. He was in a hurry for us to get the boat out.

When we backed the truck up to the boat trailer, we discovered that the ball hitch was the wrong size. A lightweight aluminum outboard fishing boat needs no more than a 1 7/8" ball. The boat trailer was in another class. It took a two inch ball. Off we went to find a hardware store. We had brought a set of tools, primarily so we could put on the new license plate. We switched hitch balls.

The boat on the trailer was pretty well balanced. Ralph and the captain had no trouble lifting the tongue onto the hitch. It didn't occur to us that it should have been heavier.

When Ralph tried to hook up the trailer lights, he shook his head. "The connectors don't match," he said. "Wrong pigtail."

Off we went again, this time to buy connectors for the lights. I have more patience with that kind of job and let Ralph stand behind the trailer to tell me if the left light flashed when I put on the left turn signal, and not the other way around.

The side lights on the trailer didn't work. Though the tail lights could be removed for launching, the side lights were permanent and the bulb sockets had corroded. A nail file helped, and I got one to work. I just hoped we would get the rig home before dark.

We did not want to be on the road at night. We had once rented a U Haul trailer and studied their tips for trailering. There was three times the chance of an accident at night. Some drivers are impatient with slow-moving trailers. Certainly no one was expecting to meet a slow-moving sailboat on the freeway in the dark. That would be enough to confuse any drunk driver.

I saw to it that the safety chains were crossed under the hitch so if our new ball came loose, the trailer tongue couldn't drop onto the highway, yanking the hitch loose in a shower of sparks. We weren't ready for that kind of drama.

Then we loaded the outboard motor, setting it gently down in the cockpit. The six gallon gas can followed. It was still full, and heavy.

"The tires look a little low," I said. "We better pump them up at the first gas station."

We were ready-- or so we thought. Everything was tied down. Nothing looked like it would fly out. Except for one yellow side lamp, the lights worked. The mast was tied securely in its cradle and the rigging wires were carefully coiled and tied in place.

"Wait!" the captain called to us as we got in the truck. He disappeared and came running up with the rudder. It had still been in his garage.

"Thanks," Ralph said as he gently laid the rudder down in the back of the pickup. "We wouldn't have sailed far without that."

"I hope we haven't forgotten anything else," I said.

Ralph started the engine and very slowly gave it gas. The truck wouldn't budge. Then, suddenly, it bounced and we were off. Looking out the window I realized we had not pulled the chocks out from the trailer wheels and had simply driven over them.

I didn't have long to think about that, because when we got to the bottom of the driveway and started to turn, the whole truck swung around with a squeal of tires and a crunch "Now what?" Ralph asked, and shut off the engine.

The captain by now was glad he had our certified check duly deposited. He was standing on the sidewalk with his eyes covered.

Ralph and I came out to survey the situation. The rig had jackknifed. When the pickup turned, the heavy boat trailer didn't, but rolled down the driveway and pushed the truck around.

The captain stood behind us with a grim expression. "Negative tongue weight," he said.

Then I realized that the weight of the outboard motor and gas can was too far back. I remembered the U Haul manual. Ten percent of the weight of the trailer had to be on the tongue. We needed a couple of hundred pounds of tongue weight. Otherwise, as had just happened, the trailer could lift the back of the towing vehicle and throw it out of control.

"Look at it this way, Ralph," I said, as we shifted the heavy gas can into the forepeak, moved the anchors out of the lazaret and into the bow, and struggled with the outboard motor to move it forward in the cabin, padding it with cushions and fenders so it wouldn't mar the varnished woodwork, "it could have been worse. It could have happened on the freeway at forty-five miles an hour in front of a gasoline truck."

"This isn't our day, Irma."

With the load shifted, the trailer sat firmly in place   on the hitch. Fortunately, it was equipped with hydraulic surge brakes. We would learn later that though hydraulic surge brakes survive immersion in water better than electric brakes, surge brakes only work to help you stop when moving forward, not when backing down a launch ramp. That's another story, too painful to tell here. Laurel and Hardy would have envied the comic potential of that routine.

That was only the beginning of our adventure. I was glad we had an early start. Though we added air to them, I was nervous about the tires. Just when I was remembering that we had no spare, one of the trailer tires went flat on the freeway. Naturally, Ralph's truck lug wrench was the wrong size. And we had no jack for the trailer.

I held up the lug wrench as a sign of distress and a trucker stopped. He showed us that it was possible to pull the trailer onto soft ground, and block it with rocks and logs so it would stay up when the flat tire was wrestled off. That didn't do the lug bolts any good.

With no spare, the flat would have to be taken in for repair. I wasn't about to be left as a damsel in distress on the highway. It's not safe.

With Ralph hanging his two hundred pounds on the stern of the boat, I could just lift the trailer off the hitch. Then I left Ralph to guard the boat while I drove the pickup to the next exit and a gas station to buy a lug wrench and get the flat fixed. They didn't have a scissors or hydraulic jack, but I knew what to do.

Ralph was bored with waiting, and cold.

"Any problems?" I asked.

"A couple of girls wanted to take me to Las Vegas in their convertible, but I turned them down."

"That's a better offer than I would have gotten," I said. "Did you dig the hole?"

Ralph displayed a pair of dirty hands. "Yep." When inflated, the diameter of the tire was bigger, but the truck driver had explained that we could dig a hole in the soft ground and put the tire back on. It worked.

It could have been worse. The trailer bearings needed repacking, but they held up until we got home just before dark.

A representative of the neighborhood neatness committee, Mr. Holzkopf, was already parked across the street when we pulled up to the house. "There's an ordinance against storing boats or trailers in front of the house," he said.

Holzkopf had already been after us because of the little, aluminum boat, which we often left in the driveway. Ralph's truck, with the camper loaded, was too high to get into the garage, but didn't count as a trailer. That bugged Holzkopf.

You don't have to be wealthy to own a 23 foot 1973 $4000 used sailboat, but some people just can't stand what Holzkopf calls conspicuous consumption of wealth. "We're parking it, not flaunting it," I told him.

But I admitted to Ralph, "We can't park in front. Holzkopf and the neatness committee will get an injunction or something." I sighed. "There go my rose bushes."

We tore up the lawn and ran over two rose bushes, backing the boat alongside the house and into the back yard. If Holzkopf says a boat in the back yard is flaunting affluence, he can dismantle his swimming pool.

Getting the camper raised on its sunken posts and back onto the pickup took us well into the evening. When we were done we were both exhausted.

We stood outside for awhile in the thickening darkness and admired the boat. Ralph wiped the transom, gauging the size of the letters of the name we would attach. "Dreamer."

"Let's go inside. It's getting cold."

Ralph settled in the kitchen and toasted me with a glass of Moosehead Lite. "Think of it, Irma, we're real yachties now."

"Yes." I was making a mental list: spare wheel and tire and two jacks: one for the tongue of the trailer, and another in case of a flat. Next time we would be prepared.

Before we drove the trailer again I would clean and repack the bearings. It should be no more difficult than the time I put a new seal under the dishwasher spray arm. But for the boat trailer I would also install a set of Bearing Buddies. They cost less than a set of bearings. Those marvelous Bearing Buddies hold a supply of grease under pressure, so if a warm trailer wheel is submerged to launch the boat, the sudden cooling doesn't suck salt water into the bearing. There's always enough grease, and you can easily check by pressing on the spring-loaded piston.

Ralph had plans, too. "We can wrap the tires with garbage bags during the winter to protect them from sun and ozone."

"I guess the captain was glad to see the end of us after that bad start." I remembered how eager he was for us to leave. "The tarp! We were supposed to get the tarp."

I had made such a careful list but had forgotten the tarp. The captain's load of stuff bound for Nebraska was snugly wrapped with the heavy canvas cover that should have come with the boat.

Ralph shook his head. "I guess you can never be smart enough," he said.

I felt badly. A good tarp would be expensive.

"Don't take it too hard, honey," Ralph said. "We got the boat home, didn't we?"

Two weeks later I had a surprise, a note in the mailbox said there was a COD package down at UPS. Ralph picked it up. It was the tarp.

"We don't have the captain's address, but the post office could forward mail. I sent him a note," Ralph explained. "I said we realized he needed our tarp for his move out west, and since he wouldn't be moving again for a couple of years, he could return it COD. It's a little tattered from the wind, but still serviceable."

"You didn't tell me you wrote."

"Heck, Irma. If he didn't send it, I didn't want you to be disappointed."

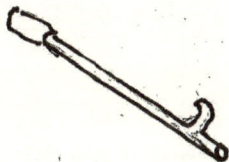

Chapter 9

BACK TO SCHOOL

One of the joys of boating is that it offers so much. The home carpenter can build herself a boat. The radio ham can have a floating platform for telecommunications. The astronomer can navigate by the stars, sun, and moon. The oceanographer can study bodies of water, currents, and tides. The beach comber can find new places to gather treasure. The engineer can tinker with gadgets. The weather watcher can record barometric pressures, winds and clouds. Those are just the beginning. There is always something new to learn.

Boating is a whole world. Running a boat isn't like buying a used car, getting in, and driving. The water is a different environment. Just think, two thirds of the world is covered by water. There's water from our marina all the way around the world.

There's so much to learn that it's a bit overwhelming. That's why Ralph and I decided to take a Coast Guard Auxiliary course in Boating Safety and Seamanship. Ralph saw an ad in the local shopper advertising classes in boating and we signed up.

The classes met at the local community college. It had been a long time since either of us was in a classroom and we felt out of place. There were about twenty people there-- a man and his teen-aged daughter, a young couple, and two women whose husbands were boaters. There was a high school teacher who I thought was a sculptor, by all the white dust and paint on his clothes. It turned out he was building a ferrocement boat in his back yard. A dentist and his pregnant wife were taking the course as preparation for the first season on their new Dutch sailboat. Then there were me and Ralph, trying to look salty in his Greek fisherman's cap.

The teacher was a naval reserve officer, but we learned that the twelve sessions would be taught by different volunteers, all members of the U.S. Coast Guard Auxiliary. Topics included safety, nautical terminology, boat handling, rules of the road, aids to navigation, marine engines, marlinespike seamanship, the weather, and use of the radio. At the end of each chapter there would be a test.

"A test?" Ralph said. "I'm not very good at tests."

"The questions are multiple guess, Ralph, like the one you take when you renew your driver's license."

"Don't remind me. I can never remember how far behind the truck to put the highway flares."

"This is a basic seamanship course, Ralph. It's voluntary, for fun and knowledge. It's not like you're getting a required chauffeur's license."

I got a kick out of the nautical vocabulary. Where else but with navigation lights would I have seen the word "occulting"? Words like garboard, larboard, inboard, outboard, and starboard had a new rhythm. There were fiddles and fids, bowline, bow line, marline, sheer line and shoreline. The possibilities of new rhymes for limericks intrigued me. During a lecture I doodled,

A homesick sailor from Brooklyne,
Was sent on a search for some marline,
When teased by the crew
And the officers, too
He said, "What I need is some shoreline."

Ralph liked the mnemonic devices, those little sayings used to help remember things, like "Red right returning" to remember to keep the red buoys on the right when returning from the sea, or "Red sky at dawning, sailors take warning," a weather watch for approaching storms.

What blew Ralph's mind were the tricks to remember corrections for compass variation. Unlike the true north pole, which stays in the same place, the magnetic pole is constantly shifting. Each nautical chart has at least one compass rose indicating the variation and the amount of annual drift. To correct for variation, Ralph memorized "East is least" and "True Virtue Makes Dull Company-- Add Whiskey." That one produces True Variation Magnetic Deviation Compass Add Westerly.

Ralph asked, "What's deviation?"

The instructor explained that magnetic deviation was the effect on the compass of metal objects aboard the boat. An inboard engine with a cast iron block would gradually align itself magnetically to the earth during winter lay up. The effect on the compass would vary, depending on the direction the boat was headed. Another source of deviation might be a magnetic object left in the wrong place, like a tool or a beverage can left on the dash or on a shelf behind the compass.

I nudged Ralph. "That's why you drink beer in aluminum cans."

"I knew there had to be a reason: beer in aluminum cans helps me keep my bearings. Very good."

We learned there were actually three bearings: true north, magnetic north affected by annual variation, and the bearing the compass showed, affected by deviation peculiar to the boat.

What seemed reasonable in the class became gibberish when we did our home work and studied for the test. "True Variation Magnetic Deviation Compass Add Westerly should be NTSRT," Ralph said.

"What's that?"

"Never The Same Result Twice. No wonder the Vikings didn't use compasses," Ralph said in despair. "They couldn't figure all that stuff out."

"Not true, Ralph. The Vikings lived in the bronze age. No iron to throw off a compass-- if they had one."

"I thought they were men of iron."

"Very funny, Ralph."

We passed the compass test, thanks more to intuition and good guesswork. Later we tried to make our own compass deviation card and found that there wasn't enough magnetic material close enough to the compass to make much difference. Besides, our small boat compass isn't that great. It reads in five degree increments. A bigger boat with a binnacle and a compass with a large card would be better. The motion on a small boat is so erratic that it's hard to steer a course within one or two degrees. It's the difference between what you can do theoretically on a stable platform and what really happens when the boat is rocking and rolling.

By the time the twelve weeks were over we felt comfortable with many aspects of boating we hadn't really thought of before. Of course, we didn't know everything. Neither of us was certain of what combinations of ships' lights at night might be shown by a tug pulling a barge, and how they might be confused with something else. We would practice SCAV: Stay Clear of All Vessels. The course was only an introduction, a starting place for real, serious knowledge.

We got all dressed up for the graduation ceremony. Not all of us finished the course. The dentist's wife dropped out to have her baby. The daughter in the father-daughter pair dropped out because her boy friend was into off-road vehicles, not boats. The man building the ferrocement boat stuck with it. For graduation night he wore something that wasn't full of paint and cement. Ralph put on his blazer. We all received our Coast Guard Auxiliary diplomas.

It turned out there was a cash bonus for taking the course. Our agent gave us a ten percent discount on our marine insurance. It seems that people who take a course in boating safety and seamanship are less likely to get in trouble on the water and file a claim.

Chapter 10

CAPTAIN OLESON'S SEXTANT

In these days of electronic wonders like GPS which is navigation by space satellite, and the already obsolete LORAN, which stands for LOng RAnge Navigation, you have to marvel at the Vikings who were able to sail open boats from Norway to North America without so much as a compass. Imagine, setting out in an open boat, cooking on an open fire laid on stones, bailing constantly, steering by the stars, and living on lutefisk.

Lutefisk is dried cod that has been soaked and reconstituted. Norwegian Minnesotans eat it at Christmas and tell jokes about it the rest of the year. Any Viking who can cross the Atlantic in an open boat on a diet of lutefisk has to be heroic.

By today's standards, Viking navigation was pretty crude. Like sailors after them before the problem of longitude was solved they would sail north or south until they reached the right latitude, then west, hoping they didn't hit any rocks in between. No diagonal short cuts on what we call a rhumb line. Though they had no sextants for "shooting the sun" they are reputed to have had a polarizing crystal that could show the direction of the sun even on overcast days.

Today even a modest yacht bristles with antennas and electronic gear. Instead of a bit of yarn on a shroud to show the direction of the wind, there are electronic wind speed indicators on top of the mast and liquid crystal displays on the instrument panel to show relative wind speed and direction.

Columbus might have carried a chip log, a knotted string with a float dropped overboard to estimate speed by counting knots, but now you can have your speed through the water measured electronically in hundredths of a knot! In the olden days depth was measured with a hunk of lead on a line. The lead had a little socket in the bottom which, armed with sticky stuff, could pick up a bit of the bottom so the sailor could tell if the bottom were mud or shells.

Then came SONAR depth sounders that flashed a little red light. They've been replaced by devices that not only display a picture of the contours of the bottom in color, but show little pictures of the fish and tell how deep each fish is!

The lowly radio direction finder was used to take bearings on radios sending signals from lighthouses. The navigator would aim the antenna to point at each source, note the direction, and then plot the lines on the chart. Where the lines intersected was where the boat was supposed to be. At best all you got was a triangle called a "cocked hat" and the boat was somewhere inside it-you hoped.

This was not easy to do in a bouncing boat. The best bearing you could get was within five degrees, and that angle multiplied by fifty miles got pretty vague. You don't see radio direction finders in the Goldstein Marine catalog any more.

The radio direction finder was outdone by LORAN. LORAN works by automatically triangulating the boat's position by calculating the time it takes for signals to reach the boat from five different land-based radio transmitters. It's the electronic version of the captain caught in fog who blows the ship's whistle, then listens for the echoes off the sides of the channel. If both echoes reach the bridge at the same time, the ship's in the middle of the channel.

With LORAN each transmitter sends a signal and the time it takes for that to reach your boat tells the LORAN how far you are from the transmitter. LORAN automatically compares the signals and shows your latitude and longitude on the screen. It can also tell you the speed over the bottom, how long at current speed it will take you to get to your chosen preset waypoint, and what course to steer for it.

The problem is, land masses can deflect the radio signal, and LORAN may not be more accurate than a couple of hundred yards. That's still a great improvement over a hand-held sextant which can be used to calculate a ship's position within only four miles. While navigating in fog with rocks all around, missing the channel by a few hundred feet could cost you your boat.

We have a LORAN on our boat. Ralph bought a used one, complete with antenna and the manual at a boat swap down at the yacht harbor, then made me wriggle back under the coaming to hold the nuts while he bolted the fold-down antenna near the stern. I don't know why he does these things.

LORAN is gradually being phased out. GPS is more accurate. It works off orbiting satellites placed 10,000 miles above the earth, a distance where the orbiting satellite appears to be stationary. GPS can show your location within a few feet!

Then, if you have deep pockets for the expense, there's radar. In order for yachtsmen to see in the dark or in fog, some motor sailboats are built with arches over the stern to raise radar antennas high enough so they won't microwave the helmsman's head.

What started out as clean-looking boats look like something the Soviets euphemistically called a fishing trawler: enough antennas to spy on the entire US Navy. We don't have radar on our boat. How much of that electronic stuff could we run on that twelve volt battery?

Imagine my surprise one Saturday afternoon when Ralph came home with a strange instrument.

"What's that?" I asked him.

"A sextant," he said, with some awe in his voice. "It's a plastic one for practice. I borrowed it from an old guy I met at the boat yard, Captain Oleson. He's showing me how to use it."

"He must be pretty trusting, loaning you a valuable navigation instrument."

"Hey, I'm not a total klutz, even if I did use a pipe wrench to twist the faucet handle off the bathroom sink."

"What are you going to do with a sextant? Sail around the world?"

"No. Captain Oleson says a sextant is useful for coastal navigation. Once I get good at that, he may show me how to find where we are anywhere on earth, just using this." He held up the instrument. "Pretty fantastic. And no batteries. Captain Oleson says people rely too much on electrical stuff."

"How does it work?"

Ralph took a deep breath and went into his wise old man mode. "Actually, all a sextant really does is measure angles. But it measures them very accurately, to the tenth of a minute of a degree. It has to be that accurate, because if you're measuring the height of the sun above the horizon, an inaccuracy could place you miles and miles away from your true position."

Ralph went on to explain that the sextant had two mirrors. One was silvered on only one half, so when you looked through the eye piece you could see the horizon through one half and the sun or a star in the reflection. By bringing the reflection of the celestial object down to the horizon, you could measure the angle on the sextant's scales. He took me out on the patio to demonstrate.

"But we can't see the horizon from here," I said.

"Right. You have to have enough flat water, about three miles of it, so the curvature of the earth begins to be noticeable. Then you have a true horizon."

"I still don't see how that can help in coastal navigation," I said.

"Well," Ralph began, and started over. But he didn't understand, either. "I've only had one lesson."

"When do you see this Captain Oleson again?"

"Tomorrow afternoon. He's retired. He hangs around the boat yard and does a few odd jobs. Why not come along?"

Captain Russell Oleson reminded me of one of those salty wood carvings you see in the souvenir shops. He walked with his legs wide apart, like a man used to balancing on a rolling deck. He wore a wool watch cap and a threadbare pea coat that hung from his shoulders like it once belonged to someone who weighed thirty pounds more. His face was thin and he looked ill. "Are you interested in navigation?" he asked me.

"Ralph says a sextant measures angles," I said. "I was always good at math. But how does something made for measuring the angle of the sun help with coastal navigation?"

Oleson was happy to have an audience. "You can measure distance off by vertical angle, like a lighthouse, for instance, or a headland. And you can use horizontal angles on three landmarks to find your position on a chart. Taking the angle of two landmarks plus a magnetic bearing will work, too."

Using the plastic sextant, he showed us on a chart he had in his car. I recognized our familiar lighthouse on the chart and understood the principal right away. Measuring the distance off by vertical angle required simple trigonometry, using the tangent of the angle of observation in a right triangle.

"But you need to know the height of the lighthouse," I said.

Captain Oleson smiled. "Right. It's in the light tables. You can work it the other way. If you know your exact position you can calculate the height of an object, like that power plant chimney." He pointed to the distant power plant chimney with its strobe lights. "The chimney isn't in the tables, but once you calculate its height and enter it on your chart you can use it for navigation, too."

He showed us where he had marked the height of the power plant chimney on his chart, then measured the angle and found the distance on a photocopy of a "Distance by Vertical Angle" table.

"Hey," Ralph protested. "Isn't using a table cheating?"

"You can work it out mathematically," Oleson said, "But a table is quicker."

I asked him where he found the table. Captain Oleson's eyes shone. "In Bowditch. The proper title is American Practical Navigator but everyone just calls it Bowditch. He was the great-grandson of a sea captain who lost a ship on a ledge outside of Salem, Massachusetts. Young Bowditch was physically so small and puny he couldn't go to sea as a regular seaman, so he worked at a ship's chandlery. He became a wizard at mathematics and was eventually able to serve as mate. It was his contention that every crewman could learn navigation, and he taught everyone aboard his ship, even the cook. At Christmas in 1803 after a long voyage and with only one glimpse of the sun in bad weather, Bowditch brought his ship safely into Salem's harbor."

Captain Oleson's voice quavered. "Can you imagine, a crew at sea for a year, expecting to lie off shore over Christmas because of bad weather. Everyone socked in on shore tucking themselves around a Christmas dinner and in sails Bowditch! It must have seemed a miracle!"

Ralph was inspired. He ordered the two volumes of Bowditch from the US Government printing office and studied them like a bible. Using Captain Oleson's practice sextant, Ralph would measure chimneys, steeples, trees. He kept a chart in the car and was forever taking detours along the coast so he could practice. I did it, too.

Celestial navigation was more complicated. Captain Oleson explained that the sun is always directly overhead someplace on earth, and that place is called the Ground Point, or GP. But the Ground Point is always changing because the sun's position moves about fifteen degrees an hour. One has to know the exact time of the observation to the second. Then there is the observed angle of the sun above the horizon, and the azimuth, the direction toward the sun, and calculations of latitude based on whether the Ground Point of the sun is above or below the equator. It was all very complicated.

One afternoon I caught Ralph on the patio, squatted down in a contortion with his back to the wall of the house with the sextant in his eye.

"What are you doing?"

"I'm shooting the sun."

"But you can't see the horizon from here. You have to measure the angle to the horizon."

"I bought an artificial horizon. See?" On the patio there was a little plastic tray with a couple of filters. "You see the reflection of the sun through the filters."

"I don't see anything," I said.

"You got to stand over here." Soon I was scrunched and contorted against the wall. I looked through the sextant.

Ralph had flipped on the dark filter so you could look at the sun without destroying your retina. Through the nearly opaque filter was the sun. I blinked. There was a little black dot on it.

"I see a sun spot," I said.

Ralph looked. "Gee. You're right. I never saw a sun spot before."

Ralph went to the public library and borrowed the Nautical Almanac and Ephemeris tables that showed the GP, the Ground Point, of the sun for every moment of every day of the year. Practice, practice, practice. Ralph was using up all the scrap paper in the house with his calculations.

"Aha!" he exclaimed one day. "I'm catching on, Irma. I've got a position. Latitude and Longitude."

"What a relief. I was afraid our patio was misplaced. I was going to call the contractor and sue."

"Very funny. Look at this." He got out the atlas and checked the latitude and longitude on a map of the world. He re-worked his calculations. Finally, subdued, he announced, "I've got serious news, Irma. Our house is in southern Quebec."

"My God, Ralph, we've been passing the wrong money at the grocery. We should have been using Canadian dollars."

"I'll have to show Captain Oleson my calculations on Sunday and find out what I did wrong."

"Why don't you settle for navigation with horizontal and vertical angles? You don't really have to be able to use the sextant with the sun and stars, not unless we go to sea."

Ralph's eyes twinkled. I think he imagined distant tropical shores. "Maybe we will go to sea. Some day."

Captain Oleson didn't show up for our lesson on Sunday. We called his house and his wife said he had died. Hadn't he told us he had cancer? That explained the weight he had lost. The cancer had spread to his pancreas and he went into a sudden diabetic coma. Captain Oleson had come to those Sunday sessions with Ralph and me because he wanted to pass on what he had learned to someone who appreciated the knowledge.

Subdued, we drove to the Captain's home to return the borrowed, plastic sextant.

"So you're Ralph and Irma Quarterdeck," Mrs. Oleson said at the door. She was a small woman in a faded blouse. Her face showed the tired lines of worry that had worn her down during her husband's illness. "Russell was always talking about you two. Come in."

The small house was full of pictures of ships, including a framed photograph of a World War II liberty ship over the mantelpiece. "Russell was First Mate then. It was sunk out from under him," he wife explained. "We'd just been married. In those days the Merchant Marine lost something like forty percent of the fleet to enemy action. You never knew if he'd come home again." Remembering, her breath caught. This last departure was final.

She regained her composure. "Russell wanted you to have something." She left the room and we stood embarrassed and uncomfortable. Mrs. Oleson returned with a teak box and handed it to Ralph. He opened the bronze latches and looked inside.

"I... I can't accept this," he said hoarsely.

"Our daughters have no use for it, and our grandchildren would only take it to pieces. He wanted you to have it."

It was Captain Oleson's sextant. Not the plastic one he had lent Ralph for practice, but a real one, one of those fine instruments you see enshrined behind glass cases in ship's chandleries.

"It's a bit old fashioned," Mrs. Oleson apologized. "The newer models are easier to use, but in the war it got Russell to Murmansk. It was the only thing he rescued off the ship when it was torpedoed."

"He never mentioned that," I said softly, remembering Russell Oleson's sea stories.

"It was terribly cold. Some of the men in the lifeboat died," Mrs. Oleson said. "Russell always felt badly about it. He had wanted to bring them all back. He didn't like to talk about that."

Ralph fumbled with the latches on the sextant case.

"Keep both the sextants," Mrs. Oleson said.

When we got to the car, Ralph said, "You drive. I'm having a little trouble with my eyes."

I think that sextant is Ralph's most precious possession. Even though we have LORAN, he uses the plastic one for coastal navigation, for practice, he says, in case our battery goes dead.

He has given up trying to find our position by measuring observed angles of celestial bodies-- at least for the time being.

"I'm no Viking who can sail by the seat of his pants," Ralph says.

"You're no Russell Oleson, navigating a lifeboat off the coast of Norway, either," I told him, "but aren't you glad you don't have to be?"

Don't tell Ralph, but I've been squirreling away some extra cash and watching the Goldstein Marine catalogs. Those GPS hand held gadgets are coming down in price and some come with built-in maps. Next time Ralph refuses to ask for directions when we're driving someplace I may be able to tell him our exact latitude and longitude. Russell Oleson would be impressed.

Chapter 11

RALPH'S BANANA FINGERS

Ever since I tried melting margarine in a covered pot I've been leery about fires. I lifted the lid to see how it was doing and poof! a great cloud of flame and black smoke! I learned later that heated oils reach a flash point where they simply explode. In that instance, I did the right thing by putting the cover back on the pot to smother the flame and removing the whole business from the burner to cool down before I dared lift the lid again.

I was lucky with the margarine pot. If I had panicked and run, the house might have burned down. When Ralph saw me he said, "Are you trying out for a minstrel show or did you have a fire?"

"A little fire," I admitted, and started to wash the soot off my forehead. "We better put a fire extinguisher in the kitchen."

In our camping days we carried a pressure can fire extinguisher filled with carbon tetrachloride, that is, until we found out that during a fire the stuff created a poison gas. Those are outlawed now.

Ralph picked up a dry powder fire extinguisher on sale at the hardware store for about twelve dollars and mounted it inside the kitchen doorway. The powder inside it is basically bicarbonate of soda, and I keep a large box of baking soda by the stove just in case.

I think something like my margarine accident may have happened to that nice Dr. Singhe. One day when we came down to the marina there was a crowd around an ambulance, a lot of commotion, and smoke in the harbor. A small cabin cruiser was burning fiercely. It burned to the waterline, then sank.

We learned later that it belonged to Dr. Singhe, one of the partners at the HMO medical center. His wife, who survived the fire along with their daughter, said that the engine had been acting funny. Flooding and backfiring. Something wrong with the fuel pump. Her husband had opened the engine cover and there was an explosion. He was blown out of the boat. Mrs. Singhe was burned badly.

Gasoline leaking onto a hot engine was just waiting for air to set it off, just like my pot of margarine. Only Dr. Singhe didn't get a chance to put the engine cover back down. Poor man. It only takes one mistake.

'Dreamer' came with a dry powder extinguisher mounted just inside the companionway hatch. It's a red, pressurized cylinder with a nozzle, a trigger, and a pressure gauge. We took it for granted until Dr. Singhe blew up. When the ambulance had driven away and what was left of the Singhe cruiser sank, we left the crowd and got aboard 'Dreamer'. The first thing Ralph did was check the fire extinguisher.

"The pressure's low," he said. He took the extinguisher off its mount and looked at the tag. "How often are these things supposed to be recharged?"

"The Coast Guard says once a year."

"Oops. I hope we don't get boarded today. We'll have to recharge this."

I made some phone calls later and found out who services fire extinguishers. There's an outfit called Safe-T. They sell all types and also sell burglar alarms.

Business must have been slow in the Safe-T fire extinguisher business because when we got there the only person in the place was sitting on a stool behind the counter and playing an acoustical guitar. He wore coveralls with the company logo and the name "Francis" sewn over the pocket. The heavy, gold chains around his neck and the guitar suggested he had a life beyond fire extinguishers.

Ralph asked, "What do you charge for refilling a dry powder fire extinguisher?"

Francis put down his guitar. "Fifteen bucks."

"But you can buy a new one on sale for twelve."

"What do you want? Life insurance or a bargain? Why don't you sit down and watch our videotape?"

Over in the corner Safe-T had a TV set up. Ralph and I watched a fire prevention program that demonstrated in flaming graphics that your best chance to put out a fire is in the first minute. If you can't, then get out. But if you have a fire on a boat, "getting out" means abandoning ship. This is not a happy prospect.

I kept seeing Dr. Singhe's boat in flames and his widow getting first aid on her hands and face.

We found out from the tape that there are three types of extinguishers, A for solids, B for liquids, and C for electrical fires. The idea behind some fire extinguishing methods is to smother the flames. That's what the dry powder types are for.

Another way to smother a fire is with Halon. Those can be mounted inside an engine compartment. When triggered by heat, they fill the compartment with Halon, a noncombustible gas. Dr. Singhe might have been saved by a Halon extinguisher.

The old soda-acid extinguishers consist of a few gallons of water mixed with baking soda and a bottle of sulfuric acid. Turn them over and the acid spills. The acid causes the baking soda to fizz, providing the pressure to squirt the water out. That cools a fire down, but the acid and soda in solution conduct electricity. Using a soda-acid extinguisher on an electrical fire could be a shocking experience.

Looking at the video, I couldn't imagine a bulky soda-acid extinguisher on 'Dreamer.' In rough water the plug on the acid bottle might bounce out and set the thing off.

Francis had gone back to his guitar while we watched. When the tape was over he shut off the machine. "Now, what can I sell you? Halon? "

That was the most expensive. "Our boat has an outboard motor. The gas can is stowed in a vented lazaret." It wasn't like Dr. Singhe's cruiser with a closed, inboard engine compartment. "Halon is one of those gases like Freon that disrupt the ozone layer." Halon can put out a fire in a closed compartment, but you can't breathe it. I didn't want it in the living space.

"How about CO_2?"

CO_2 extinguishers smother flames, too, but are pretty large. "I don't know where we could put one in 'Dreamer's tiny cabin." We had trouble enough living with Ralph's boom box.

"You're hard to please, lady."

"I'm just being practical."

"What's your most likely fire danger?"

"The galley," Ralph said. "Especially if Irma melts margarine on the stove."

"Be nice, Ralph. That won't happen again."

Ralph wasn't in the mood to spend a lot of money. He showed Francis our dry powder extinguisher. "Can this be recharged?"

"I wouldn't bother," he said. "These nylon fittings aren't very good. If they are cross threaded they won't hold the pressure. I can give it a little more gas, but I don't guarantee it will hold."

He screwed a pressure hose on the nozzle, took out the safety pin, and expertly gave the fire extinguisher a little boost. Now the needle on the gauge showed in the green.

"Pressure's not the only factor," he said, as he replaced the pin. "The powder can cake. What you do to prevent that is to give the extinguisher a couple of bounces." He showed us by rapping the extinguisher on the floor a few times. "You should feel the powder shifting inside."

"Thanks," I said. "How much do I owe you?"

"No charge, lady. I don't need the liability. Some people think that a fire extinguisher is guaranteed to put out a fire. It's not." He fingered the gold chain around his neck. "A fire extinguisher is a little like a condom. There's no guarantee you won't get pregnant or catch AIDS. It's just an aid to prevention."

I thanked the man at Safe-T fire extinguishers for the advice. He went back to his guitar and we left without having bought anything. He was right, of course. Our extinguisher didn't hold pressure. In a couple of weeks the gauge was low again. "We should buy another one," I told Ralph. "One with metal, not nylon fittings."

"Gee, Irma. The label says it should be recharged with a kit. That should save some money. Why not just recharge it ourselves?"

"If you want to, Ralph, it's your baby. I won't touch it."

The kit consisted of a bag of fine, dry powder, a brush, a little paper funnel, and a CO_2 bottle like the kind used for air guns. By the time Ralph paid for the recharge kit and the shipping, it cost nearly as much as a new fire extinguisher.

First, the old powder had to be removed. You do not unscrew the top to do this, unless you're wearing a safety helmet, goggles, and a dust mask! It would practically explode in your face. To empty the extinguisher, Ralph took it outside, pulled the pin, and squeezed the handle. A stream of white powder spewed out on the driveway. The distance was OK for a fire aboard our boat, but the duration wasn't very long. To be useful, that extinguisher had to be used promptly and aimed at the base of the fire. You wouldn't get much of a second chance.

It made an awful mess in the driveway. Ralph hosed it off, but I could imagine all that powder in Dreamer's cabin. It would hang around in nooks and crannies for months.

Then Ralph unscrewed the top of the extinguisher and cleaned out the cylinder before pouring in the sackful of fine, white powder. It made a mess in the garage, too.

Putting in the gas was the interesting part. I watched as Ralph started to screw on the little gas cylinder.

"Ralph," I cautioned him, "the warning says to wear gloves."

That was puzzling.

Ralph got some garden gloves and turned the cylinder carefully. There was a hissing sound.

"Ouch!" Ralph exclaimed, and let go of the cylinder. "That's cold."

The cylinder was covered with frost. The sudden expansion of the pressurized gas chilled the little tube.

"There," Ralph said proudly. "See the gauge? Right at the top of the green."

"Congratulations, Ralph, you did it."

Ralph gave me a big, self-satisfied smile and took off the garden gloves. "Hey, what's happening to my hands?" The smile turned into an expression of alarm.

His fingers were as big as bananas.

"Oh-my-god! What's happening? My ring finger is turning blue."

Sure enough, his fingers had swollen so much that his wedding band was cutting off all circulation.

While Ralph stared at his banana fingers, I called the poison control center. Someone there said it was probably an allergic reaction. It wasn't poisonous, but Ralph's pores didn't like that ultra-fine powder. We washed his hands, soaked them in hot and then cold water to improve the circulation. He squeezed and flexed his fingers. After a couple of hours, the swelling went down.

"I hope you didn't breathe that stuff, Ralph."

Ralph recovered, but the man from Safe-T was right. The extinguisher just would not hold a charge. Maybe Ralph hadn't cleaned all the powder out of the threads of the plastic fitting.

I went back to Safe-T. Francis was still on the stool with his guitar as if he had never left. "You were right," I said. "I want to buy two fire extinguishers for our boat." I got the dry powder type with metal fittings that can be recharged. They were more expensive than the ones on sale at the hardware store, but, remembering Dr. and Mrs. Singhe, I don't want to take any chances.

Chapter 12

HOW WE MET THE CREATURE FROM THE BLACK LAGOON

When we just had the aluminum fishing boat, Ralph's idea of an anchor was a big coffee can filled with cement. For an eye to tie the anchor line to, he stuck a bent piece of rod or a short bit of chain in the wet cement. Any old piece of rope would do to hold it-- even a clothes line. And he didn't have much of that, just thirty feet or so, because, he said, we didn't fish in water any deeper.

"All it's got to do is reach the bottom and suck itself into the mud," he said, "just so we don't drift away from a good fishing spot." Tackle and lures were his main concern, not anchors.

We found out that there was a little more to it than that on a windy day when a cement weight sitting on the bottom just wasn't enough. We kept blowing off, even when he let out more line. The home-made anchor wouldn't hold until it hung up on a sunken log. Then Ralph couldn't get it up at all and pulled until the rope broke.

"That's OK. Anchors are expendable," he said. "That's why I made a couple of them."

"Good thing it isn't an off shore breeze, Ralph," I said at the time. "Otherwise we could blow to the other side of the lake--or to the other side of the ocean."

I remembered reading about a couple who were swimming from an aluminum boat they found on a Lake Superior beach. No oars and no anchor. Before they realized what was happening, they had blown too far from shore to swim back. Lucky for them, a freighter picked them up the next day. Imagine, freezing in your bathing suit all night in an aluminum boat! A few hours later a gale hit. They and the borrowed boat got dropped off at the Sault St. Marie locks. They were lucky.

An anchor isn't just for fishing. It's life insurance.

Except on a little river or small lake, a can of cement won't do. It isn't enough to use a real piece of rope and not a bit of clothes line. Simple as they look at first, choosing the right anchor has to be about the most complicated decision to make on a boat.

"Jeeze, Irma, look at this," Ralph said, holding up the catalog from Goldstein's Marine. "I never saw so many anchors. Danforth, CQR plow, yachtsman's kedge, Bruce, Herreschoff, navy, mushroom, folding, grapnel, and a whole list of cheap imitations."

"No concrete-filled coffee cans?"

"No coffee, but there's something called a lunch hook. I guess that's to catch your lunch in case it falls overboard."

"If you lose your lunch, you probably don't want it back, Ralph."

It certainly was confusing. I read about anchors in Chapman, and the issue got even more complicated.

For the aluminum fishing boat we could manage nicely with a ten pound mushroom anchor and a hundred feet of floating polypropylene line. That was cheap, but it would never hold our 23 foot 'Dreamer.'

I realized that it wasn't the weight of the anchor that held the boat. It was the ability of the anchor to grab onto the bottom quickly and stay put. The anchor flukes had to dig in.

Different size anchors had different holding power. How much holding power you needed depended on the boat's weight and windage. If there was a lot of rigging up there in the wind, and it was blowing, say, thirty miles an hour, the anchor had to grab the bottom with more pounds of resistance than the windage. And of course, if there were waves heaving and hauling the boat, there'd be shock load to contend with. That dictated stretchy nylon anchor line.

The anchor line, called the rode, had to pull the anchor horizontally for the anchor to claw the bottom. Otherwise, like Ralph's can of cement on a short rope, the boat would just lift it off the bottom and drift away. That meant we needed quite a bit of rope.

The formula calls for a rode up to ten times the depth of the water. Even that formula is misleading, for it doesn't include how high above the water the rode is made fast. At that rate, thirty feet of rope was OK only when the bow cleat was three feet from the bottom of the lake. No wonder we'd drifted off!

I got out my note pad and started calculating. If we got caught in a thunderstorm or gale with gusts of sixty miles an hour, what would our windage be? Four hundred pounds?

According to Chapman, in a storm our 23 footer needed an anchor with holding power of about eight hundred pounds. Obviously, we couldn't carry an eight hundred pound coffee can. Only a coast guard buoy tender could haul it up!

And if we had an anchor with a holding power of eight hundred pounds, what size rope would we need? It's easy enough to find rope with a breaking strength of eight hundred pounds, but because of stress, shock loading, and the effect of knots and splices on the strength of a rope, the working load of a rope is only ten percent of the breaking strength. So to match an anchor's eight hundred pound grip on the bottom, I calculated that we needed an anchor rope with a breaking strength of eight thousand pounds!

Ralph's eyes were wide open. "That must be one inch nylon, at least. And to anchor in fifty feet of water, we'd need five hundred feet of it. The boat isn't big enough to carry that much. 'Dreamer' is a twenty-three footer, not a seagoing tug!"

I could see compromise written all over the horizon. "That's why people don't anchor in fifty feet of water. Better go for anchorages twenty feet deep and two hundred foot anchor lines."

"We also need some chain by the anchor," Ralph said. "In case it drags over something sharp. Wouldn't want to lose your anchor and your boat because of some old beer bottles."

"That's why we don't throw beer bottles overboard, Ralph."

"Someone else might. So we need six, maybe ten feet of chain. But eight thousand pounds?" He looked up the breaking strength of chain. "You've got to be kidding. It's not even on the chart. It would have to be half inch, at least! That'll weigh a ton!"

I checked the tables. "The working load of chain is half its breaking strength, not one tenth, as for rope."

Ralph was relieved. "Ten feet of 3/8th inch chain is heavy enough. Remember my back."

"Maybe we'll just have to count on staying at the dock if it's blowing that hard."

"And to think that, because of coral, some ocean cruisers carry nothing but chain," Ralph mused. "They must have windlasses to haul it up. Think of all that weight!"

I remembered seeing some descriptions of cruising boats in Boatswain magazine. "That's why some boats have a tube so chain can be led back to the keel and not weigh down the bow."

Ralph looked over his reading glasses at me. "That little biddy cleat on the bow of 'Dreamer' would never hold. The loads you're talking about would rip it out of the deck."

The next time we went out, Ralph wriggled and wiggled way forward in the vee berth to inspect the undersides of the bow cleats. Grunting and sweating, he crawled out again. "At least they're bolted on, but the bolts aren't very hefty."

He drilled out the bases of the two bow cleats for stouter, stainless steel bolts, then mounted them in bedding compound with nice pieces of dense oak as backing plates. For good measure, he found a way to attach a turnbuckle between one of the bolts and the inside end of the towing eye used to winch 'Dreamer' onto the trailer. "That's better," he said.

It wasn't long before we got to test it. When we bought 'Dreamer' it had only one anchor, a Danforth-type about eight pounds. We sailed out around the point to a little bay where we often fish. Ralph carried the anchor and line-- it had no chain--up on the bow and let down the anchor while I ran the outboard.

We were OK, or so we thought. I got out the cooler with our lunch and Ralph's favorite beer. Gradually, the wind increased.

"I think the anchor's dragging," Ralph said.

I looked at the landmarks I'd checked when we put down the hook. "I think you're right, Ralph. How much scope did you let out?" Scope is salty talk for the ratio of rope to the depth of the water.

"About three times the depth of the water."

"Better let out some more." Except for hurricanes, seven to one is supposed to be effective.

Ralph reluctantly put down his beer and went up on the bow. He felt the anchor line. "It's vibrating. I think we're dragging." He undid the rode from the cleat and, using the cleat as a brake, let more line slip out.

Then I heard him shout, "Oh, no! Quick, start the outboard!"

"What's the matter, Ralph?"

"I've lost the anchor. I was so busy I didn't realize I'd come to the end of the rope. Oh, Jeeze, Irma. How could I be so stupid?"

He came back to the cockpit. "Damn! Damn! Damn! It's our only anchor. What'll we do now?"

I was too busy trying to steer the bow up into the wind. "Get the mainsail reefed, raise it, and go home."

Back at the marina I checked the bulletin board and took down a couple of phone numbers.

That night Ralph sat on the edge of the bed, despondent. "I can't believe I lost the anchor."

"You did it Ralph, you lost it."

He put out the light. "The line just slipped overboard."

"It's not the end of the world, Ralph."

The next morning I phoned one of the numbers. It was Harry Boz, a local scuba diver. Yes, if I remembered where it was he and his partner would go out and help us find the anchor.

We went out in Harry's motor boat. Couldn't go in our sailboat, not without an anchor.

Harry Boz is a wild character with bad skin. In his scuba gear and wet suit he looked like the Creature from the Black Lagoon. His partner looked fierce with a commando knife strapped to his calf. He reminded me of James Bond in Thunderball. At the place I pointed out they dropped backwards over the side and swam back and forth until Harry came up with the anchor line.

Ralph and I hauled it in. When we got to the anchor it looked like a big ball of seaweed. "That's why it didn't hold," Ralph said.

I remembered reading that the Danforth wasn't effective in weed. We hadn't checked the bottom. We should have anchored in sand or clay.

Harry Boz and his friend stayed down a long time. Finally Harry's face reappeared. He took off his mask and grinned. "This is a good spot. There's an outboard motor down there. And I've found you a present." He disappeared under the water and came up with the chafed, ragged end of a very slimy, smelly piece of rope. It had been on the bottom a long time. Ralph and I hauled away on it. Eventually we got to a length of rusty chain and an old anchor.

We also helped Harry Boz and his partner rescue a rather new outboard and a tackle box someone had lost.

Later, after we had hosed down the anchors, Harry explained his find. "It's a Herreschoff, a variation of the yachtsman's kedge. It drops through weeds pretty good, but you'll want a trip line on it if you're around rock."

The fee we paid him was well worth it. Now we have three anchors, each with ten feet of chain, and a spare two hundred foot rode of half inch nylon. Just in case someone I won't mention gets careless, I tied a float on the end of the rode. If it goes overboard, at least we should be able to find it again without Harry Boz.

A good anchor is too important an investment to be expendable.

Chapter 13

RALPH POLYESTERED

The idea of putting a hole through the bottom of your boat just doesn't appeal to me. I get visions of seacock handles breaking off in mid-ocean, or freezing and cracking during winter lay-up. When Ralph fixed the bathroom plumbing it had a tendency to drip. Not gush out so you couldn't pretend it wasn't happening. I mean, if water was coming down the stairs like Niagara Falls you couldn't very well pretend it wasn't there. But if it just dripped a little, under the bathroom carpet, or around the toilet, it could do a lot of damage, secretly rotting out the floor, so you wouldn't know what was happening until one day, like my friend Mrs. Born, you sat on the commode and found yourself in the downstairs hall closet.

That's why I was afraid to let Ralph put a hole in the bottom of the boat to install a transducer for the new depth sounder. I was sure that, if he put a hole through the bottom of the boat, it would leak. Not a lot. But one day we'd come out to the boat and just the top of the antenna would be sticking up out of the harbor.

When we shopped for the depth sounder we did a lot of research. Shopping for electronic gear for your boat is more important than checking out the best deal on a dishwasher. You want to make sure you buy a product made by a reliable company that stands by its warranty, not some off brand that disappears as soon as they have your money and you can't ever find a repair person or a spare part. But if your dishwasher fails, your house doesn't go into the fourth dimension, taking you with it like some nightmare from the Twilight Zone. Your boat and your life can depend on your depth sounder. It's not just another gadget for hubby's box of toys.

One thing we found out was that depth sounders can be had with two kinds of transducers. The transducer is that little electrical gizmo that sends the sound pulse down to the bottom of the ocean and picks up the signal that bounces back. It can be mounted on the transom just under the waterline, or under the boat. The transom mount is ugly, because the long wire from the transducer has to be led up and inside. It's possible to make a temporary arrangement, so the transducer is hung over the stern on a board when you need it, but that's even worse. More stuff to fool around with or lose overboard.

A permanent mount through the hull made me uncomfortable. I read about a boat struck by lightning that followed the transducer cable and burned it right out of the hull, nearly sinking the boat. I just didn't want a hole through the hull. Then I saw it is possible to mount the transducer inside a bubble filled with mineral oil. The oil provides a medium for the signal's transmission through the bottom of the boat, but won't freeze during the winter when the boat is laid up. That appealed to me, but I realized there was another problem.

Some of the strength of the signal would be lost as it passed through the fiberglass hull. The transducer sends out an invisible beam of sound like a flashlight. Some beams spread the power over a wide area. Others are tighter, like a spotlight. The wide ones see more of the bottom, but the return signal is weaker. The tight beams are stronger, but if the boat is heeled twenty degrees, the beam is aimed off at an angle and the reflected sound might miss the boat entirely. It was a dilemma.

Ralph has ingenious ideas sometimes, even if his plumbing does leak, so I asked him. "How can we mount a transducer that doesn't lose the signal when the boat is heeled?"

"Mount it on a pendulum. Swinging, like on a grandparent's clock."

Grandparent's clock, not grandfather's. I like that. Ralph is learning about sexist language. Dangling a transducer on a pendulum off the transom didn't seem very secure. "How do we do that inside the boat?"

Ralph scratched his stomach thoughtfully. "Easy. Build a water box. Hang the transducer on a pendulum inside a water box. Up in the bow under the vee berth. Gives you more warning of shallow water than if it's mounted in the lazaret."

"That's your next project, Ralph."

"Gee, thanks, Irma. Just when I was planning to wash the second story windows."

It wasn't quite as easy as it sounded. The builder had sprayed a very durable paint on the inside of the boat, and plastic resin has to bond to the hull, not to paint. There was Ralph crouched in the bow, scrubbing away with a sanding block. "You sure we can't just put a hole through the hull?" he asked, rubbing his knees. "This is hard work. I've got housemaid's knee," he complained.

"Homemaker's knee," I said. "Keep sanding. It'll get you in shape for scrubbing the kitchen floor."

"I knew you were breaking me in for some other task," he grumbled. When he was done, he cleaned out all the dust and sneezed. "This stuff is bad. You know, Irma, fiberglass dust has to be hard on the lungs. I'm glad we're not doing the whole inside of the hull." He made a show of coughing. "We'd need dust masks. Good ones."

What we needed was a little compartment wide enough at the bottom for a pendulum to swing twenty or twenty-five degrees, with sides high enough so no matter how violent the boat pitched and rolled the water in the bottom wouldn't splash out. "You better cut some cardboard templates before you start hacking at marine-grade plywood," I told him. "Better yet, let me do it." I've been cutting shelf paper and patterns long enough.

There's no such thing as a right angle on a boat. Everything's curved or odd, and it took me some time with a heavy scissors to cut patterns for the water box, but it was finally done. Ralph picked up some fiberglass cloth, polyester resin, and a cheap, disposable brush at the hardware store. Once the resin set there'd be no using that brush again.

Ralph cut the three plywood pieces with his saber saw, then had a go at assembling them in the bow. "This isn't going to work," Irma. "It keeps falling apart." But then he got some quick-setting epoxy glue-- another trip to the hardware store--that would hold the pieces in place temporarily until he could get a slow-cure epoxy filler pressed firmly into the joints. It made nice, rounded seams so the fiberglass cloth could bond without gaps and bubbles under it. He would let it cure overnight.

"That stuff stinks," Ralph said after hanging his head over the space under the vee berth. "Gives me a headache."

The messy part was still to come. The next day Ralph cut strips of fiberglass cloth with an old scissors, then mixed up some of the polyester resin with a few drops of the catalyst hardener. "This stuff is sticky," he said. He had forgotten to buy disposable plastic gloves.

By now we had newspapers all over the deck, and I was afraid there would be drips and spills of resin curing forever in the upholstery. "Use plastic bread bags for gloves," I told him. We always have a few long, plastic, bread wrappers tucked away in case we catch a fish.

The bags worked, and Ralph hung with his head in the forepeak to do all the fiberglassing in one go so it would cure as a single, bonded unit. There would be no need to paint it afterwards, for the box would be out of sight, and if it ever did leak, we wouldn't have to sand the paint off to get a repair to bond to it.

When he was finished he emerged from the confined space glassy-eyed. "That stuff smells bad," he said. "I don't feel very good."

I had opened the hatch above his head, but that hadn't provided enough ventilation. "What's in this stuff?" I picked up the resin can and read the caution, "Contains polyester resin and styrene monomer. Avoid prolonged breathing of vapor. If headache or nausea occurs, move to fresh air."

Ralph took off the sticky, plastic bags and staggered out on deck. "I feel awful."

He spent the rest of the day in a stupor on the couch. "I've been polyestered," he said, when he finally came out of it four hours later. "Makes you wonder how people who build fiberglass boats can survive. What must it do to their brains and their livers?"

After that unpleasant incident I consulted a paint specialist and bought us a respirator with disposable chemical filters. I did the finishing work on the transducer water box dressed for chemical warfare, sanding off the rough edges to the tune of an electric ventilation fan.

The water box works fine. The transducer swings as the boat heels and is always pointed at the bottom for maximum sonar return. We don't have to worry about a hole in the hull.

Ralph says, "You know, Irma, that water box gives me an idea. We could build a bigger box and cut a window in the bottom of the hull. We'd have a glass bottomed boat. I know where we can get some thick Lexan...."

"Looking for mermaids, Ralph?"

"You never can tell."

"How about if I get you a pair of swim goggles and hang you over the side with your head in water?"

Ralph thought about that. "Naw. You know how I get water in my ears."

There won't be any windows in the bottom of our boat. And whenever we do any fiberglass work, it'll be with the respirator and adequate ventilation.

Chapter 14

RALPH OVERBOARD

Ralph used to joke about the silly seaman who decided to test his crew's ability in an emergency by yelling "Man overboard!" as he jumped over the side. The crew weren't very skillful, or maybe the man's wife wanted to collect on the life insurance, but in any case the marker at the empty grave said "lost at sea." And if she had planned on collecting the life insurance, she should have made him wear a life jacket. If the body's not recovered, you have to wait seven years to collect. That's a long time to wait to get access to accounts solely in hubby's name.

Ralph's moral to that story was, "Make your man wear a life jacket when he falls overboard so they can find the body." He used to tell the story for the benefit of guests aboard. Just like on the QE2 when they have their obligatory lifeboat drill at sea, we run a man overboard drill. But Ralph doesn't jump overboard. He tosses a ratty seat cushion. We lost the good one. Then we see if the guests can retrieve it. It makes for some entertaining-- and sobering-- moments. Especially when they miss the cushion on the third pass.

Like I always tell our guests, a life jacket, now called a PFD or "personal flotation device" in Coast Guard jargon, is automatic only if you wear it. I insist. We may be the only boat on Lake Superior with that rule. Ralph complies-- now. But I'm getting ahead of my story.

Ralph wanted a macho PFD, one of those duck hunter's camouflage jobs with pockets, and he wore it open like a cowboy's vest. "It's uncomfortable to zip it," he complained.

"Lose some weight, Ralph. A couple more inches of paunch and you won't be able to find your you-know-what in the morning."

Ralph said, "I'll depend on you, Irma," and leered.

When God made Adam and Eve, She was unfair to women. I swear, the reason more men take to boating than women isn't because boys like toy boats and never grow up. It's because a man's bladder holds two beers and a woman's only half a cup of coffee. A visit to the head by a woman in a life jacket and foul weather gear is an ordeal unsuited to emergencies.

That's if your boat has a head. Sit six hours in an open fishing boat with cold, aluminum seats and a chill wind on the kidneys? Forget it. It's time somebody invented an open boat seat with a potty underneath it, something discreet for a person wearing a poncho. I'd be the first one in line.

I bet you've already figured out what happened. Yep, Ralph didn't want to sit down to pee in the head like the rest of us, so he went up on the bow. "Always downwind," he was shouting as a wave from someone's wake dumped him overboard.

Did you know that sixty percent of men drowned are found with their flies unzipped? That's the ones whose bodies are found.

I knew the drill and was alongside his life jacket in thirty seconds. Ralph wasn't in it. It had come right off when he hit the water.

The boat was drifting downwind faster than I had expected.

"Over here, Irma," I heard him gasp.

Ralph is a good swimmer, but he wasn't prepared for the surprise and the cold water. I threw him our best floating cushion, and he managed to get hold of it as I brought the boat around.

Ever try to hang over the railing of your porch and lift two hundred pounds of wet cement off the lawn? A trapeze artist couldn't do it.

Our boat has almost three feet of freeboard. In the water, Ralph couldn't even reach the coaming.

"My God, the water's cold. I can't breathe," he gasped.

I never saw him so scared.

I got a line down and under his arms so he wouldn't sink, but I couldn't get him aboard.

If a couple of strong college boys in a Zodiac rubber boat hadn't seen us and rolled Ralph over their gunwales like a dead seal I know I would have lost him to hypothermia. By the time he got aboard he was too numb to hold onto a rope. So much for our man overboard drills!

We didn't have a permanent swim ladder on the transom-- not then. We never swim off the boat. But I realized that I would never have had time to search for a folding ladder in the lazaret, not and hang onto Ralph's receding hair at the same time.

When our rescuers got Ralph aboard and left us, Ralph sat shivering, soaking wet, and pale.

I would have to distract him from going into shock. "You've lost the good cushion, you dumb bunny!"

"What?"

"Our man overboard cushion. You lost it."

"Gimme a break, Irma. I almost drowned."

"Yeh, and without a life jacket. How am I going to collect on your insurance? You men are so inconsiderate."

"Jeez, Irma..."

"Now get out of those wet clothes this instant."

"Okay, Okay." He complied.

We always carry a change of clothes to wear to a restaurant in case Ralph gets fish slime and guts on his pants. Otherwise all the harbor cats follow him around and we have to eat in the kitchen.

Since Ralph's dunking, I visited a hospital supply store and bought him a plastic urinal. I marked it with a laundry pen, "Ralph's Insurance Policy." He can use it with one hand, but never on the bow.

We also mounted a permanent boarding ladder. We found out by experience that you can't pull yourself up out of the water unless there's something firm to stand on. Our ladder can be pulled down by someone in the water.

Ralph found me a bucket. He marked it, "For Emergency Use Only." "You can use this in the cockpit, honey."

"No, Ralph. Not around the guests," I told him. I'm not that casual. "And no more emergencies! Plan ahead."

He does. Ralph bought a life jacket that fits over his paunch and always gives me a grateful look when he puts it on.

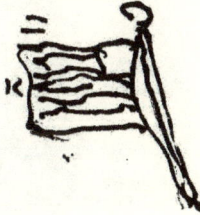

Chapter 15

MIDNIGHT MARINE SUPPLY

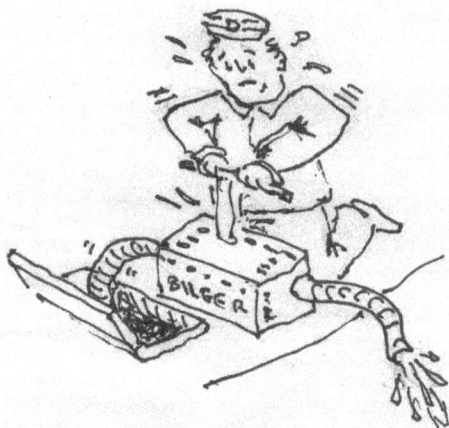

In these days of catalog shopping you can buy almost anything without leaving the house. Thanks to all those "readers' service" bingo cards in the magazines, Ralph has us on every imaginable mailing list related in any way to things nautical. We get mailers from commercial fishing supply places offering us miles of trawler gear and electronics catalogs for radars suitable for destroyers. It's an avalanche. Once you buy something you're a known purchaser. Little red flags appear in computers all over the country.

Just as I keep a file of all our warranties, invoices, and instruction manuals, habits left over from when I worked in a purchasing office, I also keep a file of the current catalogs we might actually buy something from. There's a shelf in the hall closet labeled "Boat stuff." That's to keep them separate from my Eddie Bauer, L. L. Bean, and Neiman

Marcus catalogs. Every couple of months I go through the stack and throw out those that are out of date. If I didn't, we'd be buried alive.

Ralph likes to sit on the living room floor surrounded by those marine supply catalogs. You should have seen him shopping for a bilge pump. There's a nice supply store down at the marina, Midas Marine. "They call it Midas Marine because they expect everything to be exchanged for gold," Ralph says. "At Midas Marine list price means selling price. Nobody sells for list price. That's the price put on by manufacturers so everyone can undercut it and look like they're offering a bargain."

I have to admit he's right. But there's the other extreme.

"Look at these bilge pump prices," Ralph said, showing me all the catalogs opened to the pump page. "The Gusher 25 is sold for anywhere between $90 and $46.95."

Since our boat doesn't have built-in flotation, it should have a bilge pump. Ralph's idea is to build one into the side of the foot well in the cockpit, so the helmsperson can pump and steer at the same time. He explained, "With a removable handle stowed in the lazaret, the pump needn't bash your shins when it's not needed."

"What if the handle gets lost?"

"It's not going to get lost."

"Remember Murphy's Law, Ralph. Anything that can go wrong, will go wrong."

Ralph studied the catalogs and finally settled on an off-brand pump I never heard of. It was listed in the slick, Midnight Marine catalog. In the fine print after the first blurb, it said the prices were low because Captain Black scouted around for surplus goods, picked up repossessed merchandise at auctions, and cleaned up on people going out of business. Supplies limited. Order now. I asked, "You sure he isn't Captain Black Beard, who picks up stuff at truck stops while drivers are inside drinking hundred mile coffee?"

"I don't think so, Irma. This pump is a bargain. $29.95 plus shipping. It's called the Sluicer 30. Look at the specs."

The specifications looked too good to be true. Thirty gallons a minute? How many strokes was that? And how long could someone short of Arnold Schwarzenegger keep up the pace?

"Ralph, I think a strong bucket powered by a frightened crewperson is the fastest bailing system."

But he ordered one anyway.

He told me after he sent the postal money order. "Postal money order?" I asked, incredulous.

"They don't take personal checks," Ralph explained. "Just certified checks or money orders."

"This Captain Black Beard doesn't trust anybody." In my experience, people who expect to be cheated tend to be untrustworthy themselves. "What about VISA? American Express? Master Charge?"

"Captain Black writes that by not paying the credit card companies their five per cent, he passes on more savings to the customer."

"You'll be lucky if you ever see that pump, Ralph. How much was it?"

"With the freight, thirty-five dollars."

"Did you make a copy of the order form and the money order?"

"Nope. But I have the receipt from the post office."

Three weeks went by and no pump. Ralph sent Captain Black a letter. "If you no longer have the Sluicer 30 in stock, please refund my money."

He got a card, "There's been a slight delay. Please be patient."

I knew we were in trouble.

After six weeks, a package finally arrived, $4.50 due for postage and handling. It seems Ralph had miscalculated the E-Z Shipping Rate on the table in the back of the catalog.

Looking at the table and comparing it with UPS rates, I realized where Captain Black made his profit. The low prices of the merchandise were offset by the high shipping and handling cost.

The infamous Sluicer 30 was shipped padded with crumpled old newspapers in a big, re-used carton. The pump had an instruction sheet taped to it with a crude drawing. The English was not very clear. "Service you pump." I wasn't sure if that meant that you pumped service, or if it was supposed to say 'your' pump.

Down in the corner of the instruction sheet it said, "Printed in Bangladesh." I protested. "Bangladesh, Ralph. The only thing we ever bought from Bangladesh was a cotton shirt that fell apart in the wash."

The plastic was not very robust. I've seen my share of cheap appliances-- food processors that shatter the first time you drop in a carrot, blenders whose pitchers melt in the dishwasher. The Sluicer 30 looked strong from the outside, but the underside was hollow. The seats for the mounting screws looked like they would crack under the stress of a crewperson pumping for dear life.

"How to you clean this thing, Ralph?"

"Clean it?"

"Yes, Ralph. Last time I cleaned out the bilge it was full of mushy Moosehead beer bottle labels. Those things would clog a pump in no time. Then you have to take it apart and clean it."

"The diaphragm comes off. Those little screws, see?"

"I never saw screws like that."

"Those take an Allen wrench," Ralph explained.

"You mean, an ordinary screwdriver won't take this thing apart?"

"Nope. Allen wrench."

"Do we have an Allen wrench, Ralph?"

"I got a set of them in the garage."

"You better have one in the boat, Ralph. One that fits."

He was getting uncomfortable. "Sure." I studied the Sluicer 30. From the way Ralph described it, he planned to cut a hole in the side of the foot well and mount the pump on the inside. "Inside" was way down at the foot of the quarter berth, accessible with great effort at the best of times. That meant that to clean the pump it would first have to be taken off. With all those screws to remove and replace, some were bound to roll into the presumably flooded bilge and never be found again. I could not see anybody creeping in the quarter berth head first at night without a light and fumbling with tools to clean the Sluicer 30 while 'Dreamer' threatened to sink. "You can't mount this on the inside, Ralph."

I counted the screws. Two were missing.

Ralph searched his messy work bench and finally found the Allen wrench. I removed one of the screws. "It looks rusty, Ralph." I took the screw into the kitchen. On the refrigerator I have this cute butterfly magnet that holds up my sign, "Is this snack really necessary?" I tested the screw with the magnet. "Ralph, this screw isn't even stainless steel. It'll rust tight, or the little hole for the Allen wrench will rust and nothing will turn it."

Ralph tried the magnet. "Sure enough. The screw sticks to it. Stainless steel isn't supposed to be magnetic. Maybe this is some special kind of stainless."

"Send it back, Ralph. Tell Captain Black the Sluicer 30 didn't come with all the screws. Get your money back."

Ralph sheepishly put the pump back in its shabby box. He dug out the order form. It was stamped, "Twenty percent restocking fee for returned merchandise." In the fine print at the bottom was the message, "No returns without an authorization number."

"You wouldn't have had this trouble at Midas, Ralph. You would have had immediate satisfaction, not four months of aggravation. Call Midnight Marine. They must have an 800 number."

They didn't. It was another cost cutting device. You can be sure the savings were not passed on to the customers.

Ralph tried to phone collect, but Midnight Marine wouldn't accept the call. At our expense he explained that the Sluicer 30 was missing two screws and he wanted to return it. The voice at the other end asked for a description of the screws. They would replace the missing screws at their expense, they said. What size were they?

There must be a million different kinds of screws. Flat head, round head, oval head, of all thicknesses, threads and lengths, slotted, Phillips, and Allen. There are even those funny screws you see on the hardware in public toilets, screws that can be put in but not taken out so people don't steal the hinges off the doors.

Ralph finally drove to the drug store, laid the screw down on a copy machine with the order blank and made a copy of the form with the screw and sent it to Midnight Marine.

Three weeks later we got a little envelope with a full set of stainless screws for the Sluicer 30. They had Allen heads, but were too short.

"Send that damned pump back!" I insisted.

This time I phoned. I demanded to talk to Captain Black himself. He was out, the defensive, evasive voice replied. I was beginning to think there was no Captain Black. He was just a public relations image. "The Sluicer 30 is a piece of junk. Your advertising is false and misleading. I'm notifying the postmaster general to cut off your bulk mail permit," I said.

"Okay, Okay," the voice said. "Here's an authorization number. Send it back for a full refund."

Ralph packed up the pump and sent it back by UPS. It cost him extra because the box was oversize by two inches. He was too ashamed to talk about it.

Three weeks later, instead of a refund, we got a box with another Sluicer 30. This one was cracked. Someone else had already returned it to Midnight Marine. Captain Black's henchmen hadn't even bothered to remove the letter of complaint. Some poor schnook from Houghton, Michigan wanted his money back.

I phoned again. You can bet I was steaming.

"But we refunded your money," the voice said. "The check's in the mail."

"Then why did you send us another defective Sluicer 30?" I demanded.

"Clerical error. Can't get decent help around here."

Probably don't pay their go-fers a decent wage.

"Send it back COD postage," the voice said.

To my surprise, we did get a check from Midnight Marine. Minus the twenty-percent restocking fee, minus the shipping and handling. Ralph deposited it immediately and we waited for it to bounce. Deducting the cost of phone calls and additional UPS charges, we came out with three dollars.

Then, lo and behold, there was the second pump back on our doorstep. Undeliverable. Midnight Marine no longer existed.

I got a piece of plywood and mounted the cracked Sluicer 30 like a trophy and hung it over the mantelpiece with a caption: "Next time use VISA." With VISA or some other credit card you can dispute a bill and refuse to pay. With the muscle of the credit card company on your side, even Blackbeard the Pirate has to back down.

"Take it down, Irma," Ralph said after the pump hung there a week. "You don't have to rub it in."

"Chalk it up to experience, Ralph. Think of it as a conversation piece."

"I don't want to be the butt of that story," Ralph said.

"Poor baby." I gave him a kiss, but I left the pump up.

One day when I came home from work the Sluicer 30 was gone. Ralph had thrown it out. I didn't ask about it. Any time Ralph thinks he's found a bargain with a fly-by-night company, I just say, "Sluicer 30." That's enough.

Chapter 16

A TOUCH OF THE TROPICS

Some people buy boats as status symbols, but they're so busy working to make the payments that all they manage is a few yachting weekends a summer, weather permitting. The bigger the boat, the less it leaves the dock. Many owners dream of chucking the rat race and escaping forever to some tropical paradise. Few do, but one couple we met actually has, the Paduans.

We met the Paduans a year or so ago. They were aboard a beautiful ketch named Hippocrates. Bill and Mary Paduan had managed to retire early, thanks to her inheritance and a disciplined regimen of savings in interest-bearing investments. The Paduans avoided the purchase-mortgage-payments treadmill. "You don't own a house and two cars," Bill Paduan told us over glasses of rum punch. "They own you. Not only do you have to keep working like a slave to pay for them, but you have to be forever maintaining them."

"I'll drink to that," Ralph said. He's always grousing about having to fix the stairs or get up on the roof. "We bought one of those bargain houses the real estate agents describe as 'needs minor repair.'"

The Paduans own practically nothing. They didn't even own the boat they entertained us aboard. They were delivering the Hippocrates to St. Thomas in the US Virgin Islands. The owner was a doctor who didn't have time to sail it there himself.

Bill Paduan explained that the doctor owner hardly had any time to sail at all. When he did, Bill and Mary Paduan were crew. The rest of the winter they boat sat.

Ralph leaned back against the cockpit coaming and pulled his Greek fisherman's hat down over his eyes. "What a deal. A life of yachting leisure in a tropical paradise." I wondered what fantasies were going on behind the brim of his hat. I suspected something out of Gaugin's Tahiti, bare breasted brown maidens.

"Maybe you two could join us for a week."

I was skeptical. It sounded like one of those phony invitations that never materialize, "We must get together for lunch some time." But in the middle of a blizzard we got a post card invitation from St. Thomas. The last line should have tipped me off: "Bring sun screen and something to read."

We managed to both get the week off. Fleeing a cold snap and dressed in storm coats and heavy boots, we caught a Midway Airlines flight direct to St. Thomas with a stopover in Miami.

What a contrast! Dressed in faded cutoffs, cotton shirts and floppy hats, Bill and Mary Paduan met us at the airport in St. Thomas. They looked great. Their faces were brown and their hair bleached blond by the sun and salt water.

Neither Ralph nor I had been in the tropics before. We'd gotten on the plane in the wintery Midwest, and a few hours later, here we were, a hundred degrees warmer. It was hot. We changed to summer clothes at the airport and did a little tour before going out to the Hippocrates, picking up a case of rum on the way. The sun felt like it was concentrated by some giant's magnifying glass.

"I feel like a paleface," Ralph said. "Everybody here has a great tan. Boy, will the guys at the office be jealous!"

Mary Paduan was cautious. "You got your sunscreen?"

"My druggist recommended Number 30," I said. In the days before the greenhouse effect and ozone degradation, people bought oils and grilled themselves to brown crisps on the beach. Now it's sun screen. Number 15 protects people with normal skin. I'm fair, so I have to use the maximum, number 45.

The incidence of skin cancer is increasing fast. Though the type that is isolated on the surface of your skin is 95 percent curable, moles and dark spots in the skin can turn into virulent melanomas that metastasize rapidly. Once a cancer takes off into your system, your chances are poor. So much for the joys of tanning. I prefer pale skin to a melanoma.

The Hippocrates was anchored in the harbor and we went out in the rubber tender. Ralph was like a kid at the circus. "Look at this! Fantastic! Windsurfing, snorkeling."

With our stuff stowed aboard we changed into bathing suits and had a drink in the shade of the Bimini top while Bill Paduan prepared some fish he had speared for supper.

"What did you bring to read?" Mary Paduan asked.

"A thriller," I said. "*Scratch—out!* and a sexy mystery called *Ben Zakkai's Coffin.*"

Mary approved. "Cruisers are always trading reading matter. Some paperbacks have crossed the ocean several times in the libraries of different yachts."

We settled down for the night in berths above the settees in the lounge. The big yacht rocked gently. "Ain't this great?" Ralph said. "You can live off the sea. In the morning Bill's going to show me how to spear fish."

They went off in the morning and came back with a sack of fish. The sun was already hot.

I asked Ralph, "Did you put on your sunscreen?"

"I was under water most of the time," Ralph said.

"Put it on now," I said, and smeared it on his shoulders, arms and legs. "Your nose is already red. You better wear a shirt or you'll get burned."

Ralph went up on the bow to work on his tan while I stayed under the awning. Then I heard him shout, "What country's flag has a red background and a blue and white cross?"

"That's Norway," Mary Paduan said.

A Norwegian yacht had anchored close by.

"They're all naked," Ralph said.

"Really?" I looked. Sure enough. Two handsome couples who obviously sailed in the nude. No strap marks, and tanned bottoms.

"Wow," Ralph said. "That blonde's gorgeous."

I'm in favor of healthy bodies, male and female. "There's a nice pair of buns," I said, reminding Ralph that women can ogle, too.

The rum broke out early. Ralph came back for a cool drink and returned, half crocked, to his spectating on the bow. He lay on his stomach watching as the nude Norwegians cavorted, swam off their boat, and generally put on a show. I immersed myself in the thriller and forgot about the time.

A cry aroused me. It was Ralph. He was crawling along the cabin top. "Ouch. I'm sunburned."

"I warned you, Ralph. Your ears are red. Did you put sunscreen on your ears?"

"It's my feet. I've burned the soles of my feet."

Ralph couldn't walk.

He could drop overboard into the harbor to swim, but he couldn't stand on the ladder or climb it. We had to hoist him aboard like a corpse. "You've got to lose some weight, Ralph," I said as Bill Paduan and I hauled Ralph aboard by his arms. Being sunburned in his armpits didn't help any. Ralph was a bundle of pain.

Ointments didn't help. He got some relief with a paste made of baking soda, but he couldn't walk. He crawled around on his knees. While I treated Bill and Mary Paduan to steak dinners on shore, Ralph stayed aboard and suffered, confined to the boat like a prisoner on a ration of peanut butter sandwiches.

We did get in some day sailing that week. Ralph could steer, but he couldn't move around the deck very well. Beach combing or wading were impossible. When not in the shade of the Bimini he bundled up like the Return of the Mummy on the late-late show. The only facial skin that showed were his nose and lips, coated with zinc oxide lotion.

By the end of the week, he could just hobble. He grew bored with watching the nudists on the next boat and read my books and the ones already aboard the Hippocrates. The doctor owner was a Joseph Conrad fan and had well-worn copies of *Lord Jim, An Outcast of the Islands, The Shadow Line*, and other sailors' yarns.

By the last day, Ralph had come to some conclusions about life in the tropics. "Have you noticed how much liquor they put down here? The first cool one at about ten in the morning. Then there's the afternoon, and the obligatory cocktail hour, and so on. At least five a day. That's a lot of booze. In *Lord Jim* Conrad describes how white men are destroyed by the tropics, and I can see how. Didn't Gaugin die of syphilis and booze? If we stayed around here we'd turn into rummies."

"It's not a productive life," I said. "I guess we're just full of the Midwestern work ethic. I mean, when Saint Peter asks you what you did with your life, what would you tell him? I got a good tan?"

Ralph winced. "That's not funny, Irma."

When we flew home I had to push Ralph through the airport in a wheelchair, our carry-ons piled on his lap. He looked awful. His ears had blistered and peeled. I was afraid the soles of his feet would come off. He couldn't wear his winter boots and hobbled the few yards from the baggage claim across the frozen sidewalk to the car with his feet in plastic bags. Some Charlie Chaplin wag remembering *The Gold Rush* quipped, "What'd you do, Mister? Eat your shoes?"

I was OK. In St. Thomas I had worn my floppy, white, wide brimmed hat that shaded my neck, ears, and nose. The sunscreen worked.

I have to admire Ralph for his courage. He limped grimly back to work and became the stoic butt of sunburn jokes.

Last we heard from the Paduans was a post card from Venezuela. They were crewing on another yacht. Hurricane Hugo had wrecked the Hippocrates but the doctor owner was collecting on the insurance and shopping for a bigger boat.

We're perfectly happy with ours. When it gets chilly on the water and I have to wear a heavy wool sweater under my foul weather gear I remember Ralph hobbling around with his sunburn.

Chapter 17

UP THE MAST

Our couch potato neighbors Ted and Gladys were of no use when our fishing motor was stolen out of the driveway. They're not boaters. Worse, their son Toby the Terror gets into everything. Ralph needed a ladder to get aboard 'Dreamer' when it was parked in the back yard on its trailer. Not Toby. That kid was dancing on the cabin top in a flash.

Toby is the kind of boy who discovers the split rings that secure the clevis pins that hold up the mast and takes them out just to see what will happen. This is what nightmares are made of. You'd never think he would come to our rescue. But more of that later.

It all began one Saturday when the wind came up and Ralph had to take down the genoa jib. It's not easy to change headsails on the bow of 'Dreamer.' She's only a twenty-three foot boat, and there's no proper hatch over the forepeak, just a small ventilator. Sails can't be pulled up or dumped down through it. That means whoever goes forward to take down the genoa and raise the working jib when it starts blowing too hard has his hands full. His, not mine!

There's the working jib in its sack to be lugged forward and not dropped overboard. And the genoa to haul down and disconnect while the wind tries to push it back up the forestay or into the water. All this on a bow that's heaving in the waves. With Ralph's two hundred pounds, make that plunging. It's not only a bit scary; it's also wet. With all that activity going on, it's no wonder that something is likely to go wrong.

Sooner or later it had to happen. We lost the jib halyard.

There are worse things, like sinking, losing the crew, or dropping the outboard. Losing the jib halyard also makes you feel pretty stupid.

Ralph released the halyard at the mast and went forward to haul down the genoa while I steered. Things got a bit confused. There he was, hanging onto the pulpit, sitting on the working jib in its sack so it wouldn't go overboard, hauling the genoa down, and shouting for me to take up the sheet, so the clew of the sail wouldn't hang down into the water. He unhooked all those little hanks that hold the sail on the forestay and, whoops, the genoa was overboard. We weren't going to lose it, because the sheet was still attached, and I had that safely made fast in the cockpit. But in the confusion Ralph forgot about the halyard.

He looked up and there it was, blowing in the wind. Hanging onto the stay, he stood up to reach for the shackle end as it danced in the air, just caught it, then saw the jib about to slide overboard. "Whoa!" he yelled, and sat down on the sail bag with the shackle in his hand. Before either of us knew what was happening, the halyard slipped through its block up on the mast and came down.

A stopper knot wouldn't have helped much. We would still have to get up the mast to grab hold of it. Someone would have to reeve the halyard through the block again.

This was not something we were going to do while the boat danced a merry hornpipe on the waves. Ralph may be a deck ape, but he's no monkey who can climb an aluminum mast under any conditions.

I didn't have time to think about how we were going to get the jib halyard back up. It was all I could do to fish the sopping genoa out of the water and pull it into the cockpit. Once it was safely aboard I released the jib sheet and hauled it aboard, too.

Believe me, this is not our usual way to change headsails.

Ralph crept back from the bow with the jib in its sack and the end of the halyard wrapped around his wrist. He sat with the line in a jumble on his lap. He kept looking up the mast at the block we somehow had to reach, muttering, and shaking his head.

I sailed us back with just the main. Sailing was pretty slow, but we weren't disabled.

Back at the marina we spread the genoa on the grass to dry and talked about how we were going to get the halyard back up. There were several possibilities:

1) We could take the mast down. That required removing the boom first.

2) We could forget about the halyard and sail without a jib all season, then reeve the line through the block before the mast was raised for next season's sailing. I didn't feel like waiting.

3) Ralph could climb the mast with the halyard in his mouth. Douglass Fairbanks could do it with a cutlass in his teeth, but not Ralph. Not me, either.

4) We could make a boson's seat and hoist Ralph up the mast on the main halyard. Even if we could rig a block at the rail so I could get the halyard to the cockpit winch, I didn't have confidence in my ability to haul him up.

5) We could make a boson's seat and Ralph could haul me up. Forget it. He might get distracted by some blonde and let go of the rope. Besides, I'm afraid of heights. No way was I going to swing like Spider Man and skin my shins on the rigging wire.

6) We could cant the boat. Pull it over on its side in shallow water until the mast was pulled down within reach. I was afraid it would fill with water and sink. Certainly everything stowed inside would be scrambled.

7) We could motor up beside a bridge so someone standing on the bridge could reach the mast. That was a possibility. Where was there a bridge the right height?

8) We could befriend someone working with the power company and borrow their "cherry picker" with its hydraulic lift. I even phoned and learned they wanted fifty bucks an hour. So much for friendship. And to think all these years we've bought our electricity exclusively from them! Some loyalty to customers! We rationalized that the truck that carries the cherry picker was too heavy for the finger pier at the marina. Actually we didn't want to spend the money, and we didn't want to put on a circus performance to amuse everyone at the marina or to get in the newspaper. The fire department sometimes rescues cats out of trees, but they're dumb animals. The fire department doesn't rescue dumb sailors who slip their halyards.

None of these solutions seemed very practical to me. Luckily, we were in port. What would Chichester have done if that happened to him while alone at sea? We both puzzled over ways to climb the mast. Looking through the catalogs, we discovered several methods.

We could install stainless steel mast steps. Seemed an awful lot of hardware and expense just to get a line through a block. Steel steps would also make the mast of our small boat look like something on a Russian trawler.

Someone sells a sort of webbing ladder that is hoisted up the sail track. That seemed very practical to me, but it cost a lot.

There is also mountain climbing gear, some sort of ingenious gripper that allows an athletic type to slide up a rope like an inch worm. Neither of us is athletic.

"Whatever we do," Ralph said, "We have to make sure we don't ever have to solve this again."

I tried to imagine someone going up that mast. "Toby the Terror could get up in no time."

We looked at each other and smiled. "Aha!"

Ted and Gladys' kid would put Calvin and Hobbes to shame. Toby the Terror is either hyperkinetic or juiced up on sugar snacks. I know he can climb, because I've had to chase him down out of our oak tree.

We tactfully approached our neighbors. How about a little picnic aboard 'Dreamer"? No need to hire a sitter. Bring Toby. We had a little job for him to do, if Ted and Gladys would agree.

"Just so we stay at the dock," Ted said. "I can't swim."

I packed a picnic basket. Ted and Gladys came out dressed in semi-yuppie slacks and soft Nike shoes. Toby had on a Spider Man sweat shirt. That seemed appropriate.

When Toby saw Ralph's Tee shirt he said, "Hi, Mr. Moose."

Ralph gritted his teeth. "I'm Mr. Quarterdeck to you, Toby."

"But you have a moose on your shirt."

"You have a spider on your shirt, but you don't eat flies."

I nudged Ralph and whispered, "Quiet, Ralph, maybe he does."

We all drove down to the marina in my Suburu. Poor Ted and Gladys were trapped in the back seat with the kid. When we got to the parking lot Toby was off like a shot. I was sure he'd run to the end of the pier and keep going like the coyote in Road Runner.

"Toby, come back!" Ted shouted.

I set up the picnic in the cockpit while Toby explored the boat, squealing, "Gee, this is neat! What's that for?" etc. Ralph watched him like a hawk.

"Hey, a radio!" Toby shouted and grabbed our VHF microphone. "Mission control! Mission control! Enemy aliens approaching!"

"I bet you can't climb the mast," Ralph said.

"Oh, yeh?" Toby flicked out of the cabin. He sized up the task. "How much you wanna bet? Five bucks?"

"See that little pulley up near the top? If you put the end of this rope through it for me, I'll pay you five dollars."

Toby put the end of the jib halyard in his teeth and started up the mast. Another Douglass Fairbanks, I was thinking, but he couldn't make it.

"I'll hoist you up on this seat," Ralph said, and produced the boson's seat he'd made for the occasion out of a plank and some rope.

"You sure that's safe?" Ted asked, apprehensive.

"Sure, standard equipment on tall ships."

"Then why don't you do it, Quarterdeck?"

"He's too heavy."

We clipped the main halyard to the rope of the new boson's seat and while Ralph took up on the line I settled Toby securely in it. He held the end of the ubiquitous jib halyard with one hand and the boson's seat rope with the other.

"Easy, now," Ralph said, and he and Ted hoisted Toby up the mast.

"Feed the end of the rope through that little pulley," Ralph coaxed.

"Like this, Mr. Moose?"

"Yes."

I got hold of the halyard as it came down and made it fast to the cleat on the mast. "OK! You can let him down now."

The boson's chair came down slowly, but Toby wasn't on it.

"Toby!" Gladys shouted. "Get down from there!"

Toby was using the aluminum spreader for a jungle jim. He stood on it, holding onto the stay. "Wow! This is a great view!"

Ralph hoisted the seat up again. "Get on the seat, Toby. That's a nice boy."

Toby shouted, "I'm not ready yet."

"Maybe if we just ignore him he'll come down by himself," Gladys suggested.

It's not easy to ignore a kid who's playing Tarzan half way up your mast and any second may fall down and break his neck. Raising my voice, I said, "I'll serve the chocolate cake."

Not daring to look up, I heard, "Hey, chocolate cake!" Out of the corner of my eye I saw Ted stare upward and Ralph wince. I heard the sound of skin squeaking on metal, like kids make when they slide down a playground slide.

Later Ralph described how Toby had hung from the spreader, gripped the mast with his legs, and made like a fireman on a pole. The stress of dealing with that kid was tougher than our worst boating emergency. But the jib halyard was up again.

Afterwards, Ralph puzzled over how we could prevent another occurrence of a lost jib halyard. "If we attach it permanently to a ring around the forestay, it can't swing loose," he reasoned. "And if we put a fairlead on the mast and a figure eight stopper knot at the end, it can't run up the mast."

Looking at his crude drawing, I said, "It could still ride up the forestay."

"We could use a little line to haul it down. Put a block at the bow and run the line back to the cockpit, like this." Lights went on in his head. "Instant downhaul, Irma. If the jib is hoisted from the cockpit, it could be released there, too, and hauled down with this little line. Then whoever went up on the bow to change headsails wouldn't have to wrestle with a flapping sail. The downhaul would keep it on deck."

"You're a genius, Ralph."

He shook his head. "No, just lazy. Necessity isn't the mother of invention. Laziness is. The guy who invented the wheel was just too lazy to drag all that stuff on the ground."

Laziness or genius, we haven't had to enlist Toby the Terror to go up the mast again. It's just as well. The kid's into potato chips and fries lately and is getting too porky to swing from the spreaders.

At the end of the season Ralph installed a second block on the mast for a spare halyard. In an emergency it can be used to hoist the main, or a second jib if we want to raise two headsails for a downwind run. Even if we don't lose a halyard, there's still the chance we might have to change the masthead light bulb or fix the antenna. For that Ralph made a long, narrow rope ladder with rungs just wide enough for a shoe. If he has to, and has the courage, he can hoist it to the top of the mast, tie the bottom end down so it doesn't swing, and climb that. I think Ralph made that ladder just for insurance. He doesn't like being called "Mr. Moose."

Chapter 18

ROPE

Ralph and I were watching the old movie classic, "The Black Pirate" with Douglass Fairbanks Senior. The great stunt man had just single-handedly disabled a ship full of sleeping pirates by hoisting himself to the top of the mast using a cannon as a counterweight, then sticking his sword into the sail and riding it down as it shredded the canvas. I was marveling that he did those stunts himself when Ralph said, "Colored Rope."

"What?"

"Colored rope," Ralph said. "We should use color-coded rope."

"What for?"

"Avoids confusion. Think if Douglass Fairbanks grabbed the wrong rope when he kicked the cannon overboard. He'd have drowned himself."

"What are you talking about, Ralph? The movie's in black and white."

"No, Irma. I said we should use colored rope."

"We don't have a cannon on 'Dreamer.'"

"No, but if we replace the main sheet with a red rope, I wouldn't have to tell a guest, 'Take up on the main sheet.' I could just say, 'Pull on the red rope.'"

"That makes sense." I went back to my needlepoint.

Technically, I read that there are only four ropes on a boat. There's a bell rope and a bolt rope and a couple of others. The rest are called lines or halyards or rodes, and so on. Rope shmope. To me, it's a nautical quibble.

Ralph is really into rope. I'm not talking about when he first got the boating bug and filled the bed with snippets of scratchy manila. He'd bought an assortment of fids and a marlinespike and taught himself how to splice three strand, laid rope. It was when he got confused by the messy tangle of lines at the mast of 'Dreamer' that his interest was aroused again.

Ralph wasn't sure which halyard was which-- main or jib. In the cockpit when he would try to show off in front of guests, he'd say, in his Captain Hornblower voice, "Take up a little on the starboard jib sheet."

Who knew starboard? There were no sheets or even a bed in sight. Nobody wanted a lecture on nautical terminology. Our guests just wanted a good time.

Ralph showed me the Boat/U.S. catalog. "Look at all these ropes, Irma. All colors and sizes. There's three strand and braided. Nylon and Dacron. Smooth to run freely through blocks and fuzzy so it's easy to grip. There's pre-stretched. Goldstein's Marine has braided line with a Kevlar core. The Dacron cover resists abrasion and the Kevlar core doesn't stretch. It's ten times as strong as the same weight in wire."

"So what do you choose?"

"Yes."

That was cryptic. I knew what he would buy: whatever was cheap. The gas station sells rope, too, but not Dacron. Ralph has bought what is called poly rope, polypropylene. It doesn't rot but leave it out in the sun all season and it starts to flake. I had some of that cheap stuff for clothes line once, and the weather turned it to powder. That won't do. I threw it away before it dropped the laundry on the lawn. Now my clothes line is cotton over a nylon core.

For the dinghy painter we use braided polypropylene, the kind that floats. Floating line is less likely to get caught in the propeller, and if you have to snag it with a boat hook, there it is-- on the surface. It comes in bright colors, too, like yellow, red, and blue but it's not as strong as Nylon or Dacron and sunlight breaks it down. Once weathered, the rough bits are harder on the hands than manila.

Ralph is expert at making eye splices and splicing together three strand, laid line. He even adds bits of old garden hose for protection against chafing. You can't do a short splice with braided line.

Ralph saw on the wrapper that it was easy to make an eye splice in braided polypropylene. Since it's basically a tube, you stick the end in a fid and slip it back into itself, leaving a loop. He didn't have a fid, which is a little tool that is pointy at one end to separate the yarns in a rope and hollow at the other end. I made him one by sawing off the end of a dead laundry marker at an angle, using a bread knife. He was so delighted that he searched the house and cut up half my marking pens for fids.

Ralph made the eye splice in the dinghy painter with no trouble, but braided polypropylene is slippery. The dinghy yanked and yanked on Ralph's eye splice until the loop slipped out. The dinghy banged streaks of red paint on the white hull of boat in the next slip. Not the best way to be friendly with the neighbors. Now when he makes an eye splice in braided polypropylene he stitches through it with a bit of seizing twine.

Ralph discovered how to make two interlocking eye splices, pulling the loops shut, so two pieces of braided polypropylene line are joined almost invisibly. He calls it the Quarterdeck Splice. It's not in any book. For weeks afterward he'd carry a piece of spliced polypropylene in his pocket and demonstrate to anyone who would listen. "The Quarterdeck Splice! And I invented it!" People thought he was weird.

Ralph's become an expert on rope. We took a walk along the dock and he demonstrated. There's an express cruiser there called "Mean Machine." Ralph picked up the end of its mooring line and said, "See? Three strand, laid Nylon. It stretches, so it absorbs shock, but it's getting stiff from the sunlight. Ultra-violet degradation."

Mean Machine's owner shouted, "Hey! Stop messing around with my line!"

"Ultra-violet degradation!" Ralph yelled back, like some kind of curse.

"Oh, yeh? You and who else?" The owner came over looking mad.

"Sunlight's breaking down your nylon," Ralph said. "See how stiff it's getting?"

The owner felt the rope. "Sure enough."

Ralph reached in his jacket pocket. "Ever see this? I call it the Quarterdeck Splice. Look at that."

The man listened patiently, but finally said, "I don't use braided plastic rope," and walked away.

"Better be careful who you call degraded, Ralph."

"The rope, Irma, not the man."

"Love me, love my boat," I said.

Ralph began to try my patience. Finally, one day I found a length of discarded double braided Dacron line. It had been chafed in the middle so the cover was ruined. "Splice that one, Captain Hornblower."

Ralph studied it. He hadn't tried that kind of splice before. "Hmm."

"Bet you can't do it."

"What'll you bet?"

"If you can't, you wax the kitchen floor. If you can, I'll wax your pickup truck."

"It's a deal." Ralph walked into Midas Marine and showed the clerk the rope. "How do you splice this stuff?"

I'd seen the kid behind the counter before. A tanned, athletic wind surfer with great shoulders. He sort of sneered at Ralph's piece of discarded rope. "Why don't you buy a new piece? We stock all sizes."

"It's for practice," Ralph explained.

"We have a kit." The clerk produced one and was surprised when Ralph bought it. It included a fid and a long, thin rod called a pusher.

I suggested, "If you give up, you can sharpen it and make it into an ice pick."

"I'm not going to give up." That evening Ralph puzzled over the elaborate instructions. He cut the rope where the cover was frayed. There were bits of Dacron all over the living room carpet. Ralph mumbled, "The inner core goes into the other core and the outer... Jesus!"

"How's it going, Ralph?"

"Don't ask. I'm counting." He counted and marked the yarns as per the instruction sheet.

It took him a long time. He had to start over at least twice. By ten o'clock he still hadn't figured it out.

"Time for bed, Ralph, I said. "Give up?"

"No. I'll get it." He went to bed with the instruction sheet.

Just in case he forgot, when he got home from work the next day I had the line and his tool kit laid out for him on a tray.

After supper he tried again. To get the splice smooth required pulling on the cover, "milking it down," the instructions said. The writer must have been a farmer once. Ralph milked that line so hard he had blisters on his hands. No cow would have stood still for that kind of treatment. Finally, he held up the rope. "Done!"

"It's bulgy, Ralph."

"It's supposed to be bulgy. See the instruction sheet?"

He was right. "You did it, Ralph." I gave him a big hug.

"Hug's not enough," he said. "Simonize tomorrow. Make that truck shine."

It took me two hours to shine his truck, but when I finished I discovered he had done a great job on the kitchen floor. "You were right, Irma. It was a bulgy-looking splice. Next time I'll stick to splicing three strand line."

When Ralph did replace our old main sheet he didn't get it at the gas station after all. He ordered some nice, fuzzy, red Dacron. When we installed a topping lift, he used blue line, and the line used for slab reefing is green. If there's a tangle of lines in the cockpit, they are easier to sort out.

Colored line wouldn't have helped Douglass Fairbanks with that cannon trick, though. He still had to be smart

enough to know which end of the line to grab when he
kicked the cannon overboard.

Chapter 19

RALPH'S SEA SHANTIES

There's something about tall ships that absolutely inspires Ralph. The sight of a square rigger throws him into a kind of fever. To satisfy his fascination for them, I bought him a plastic model boat kit of the Cutty Sark, but he couldn't finish it. He doesn't have the fingers or the patience to deal with all those little threads for rigging.

"What would I do with it when it was finished? Gather dust on a bookcase?" he asked. "It won't work in the bath tub. Better use those hours on a real project for 'Dreamer.'" But he sees romance in the old tea clippers racing from China back around to England. Names like Flying Cloud and Thermopylae belong to a special time in nautical history.

I remind him that there's nothing romantic about hours and hours of pumping a leaky clipper ship. Climbing tarry ratlines to take in a topsail with nothing but a foot rope between you and the raging sea does not strike me as romantic. Terrifying, yes. I remember how the German training ship Pamir was pressed down by a typhoon and lost all but six of those young cadets.

If Ralph read "The Rhyme of the Ancient Mariner" instead of Joseph Conrad, he'd see no romance in scurvy or eating your leather shoes when the salt pork and weevil-infested flour are exhausted. Those may have been the days of wooden ships and iron men, but they must have had iron stomachs!

In the days of sailing ships it took a lot of men pulling together to hoist a halyard, take in a sheet, or haul the anchor. A capstan with slots for the bars must have been devilishly hard work and it would take a song with a good rhythm to get the crew working together. No need for any of that on a boat the size of 'Dreamer,' but there is a kinship.

Maybe it's karma. Maybe we remember the experience of previous lives. Some Jungian recollection of the sound of the wind in the rigging, the motion, and the spray, the lure of the sea. We don't eat salt pork and weevil bread on 'Dreamer' and there's no ratlines or tar. What we do have is sea shanties as our link with the heroic, romantic past.

Ask Ralph to take up the anchor and he breaks out with his own version of "Haul Away Joe":

"My Irma once was young and sweet, but now she's getting lazy.

Away, haul away, haul away Joe.

She lounges on the after deck and almost drives me crazy.

Away, haul away, we'll haul away Joe."

He's made up several verses.

Hand him a bottle of his favorite Moosehead beer and he starts in with "What do you do with a drunken sailor? What do you do with a drunken sailor, early in the morning? Put him in a bunk with the captain's daughter..." and so on. That's before he finishes one bottle, and he never drinks more than two. Makes him dizzy.

It would be better if Ralph had a voice. I thought about buying him a harmonica to play sea shanties on. I told him there's something wistful about the sound of a harmonica played after sunset. I had an ulterior motive. You can't play a harmonica and sing at the same time.

Ralph settled for playing his boom box. He bought tapes of sea shanties, the bawdy kind you can't play when modest guests are aboard. Fortunately, it's not a ghetto blaster that can only be carried on the shoulder by a dancing dude. Ralph's is small enough to be tolerable in 'Dreamer's tight cabin.

He thought about making a permanent installation. "We need stereo speakers on the spreaders," he announced one afternoon.

"Why would you want to do that, Ralph?"

He wasn't listening. "I would be a tricky installation. The speaker wires would have to be run down inside the mast and out again near the bottom to a waterproof deck connector. And they'd need to be protected by grommets so they wouldn't short out."

"If you install speaker wires that hang down inside the mast they'll bang around in there. Remember the trouble you had with the radio antenna wire and lead for the masthead light? Clang, clang all night. Didn't quit until you shoved foam sponges up inside."

"If we had speakers on the spreaders we could play the overture from the Flying Dutchman when the weather got rough." He swung his arms like a conductor. "Ta dum ta ta TAAA tum," etc.

"Rough weather is dramatic enough without music, Ralph. How would you fish more wires around those sponges?"

"I guess it would be too difficult."

He sticks to the boom box and the sea shanty tapes. To make sure guests can chime in when the mood inspires, Ralph made Xerographic copies of G-rated sea shanties he found in the public library. He bound them in little, waterproof plastic binders. Now everyone can sing along with Ralph: "In Amsterdam there was a maid, and she was master of her trade, I'll go no more a roving with you fair maid."

We were in Amsterdam when we did a tour of ten European countries in six days, and I know what trade that Amsterdam maid was in. It wasn't sail making. And they didn't call it roving. I'm sure that the reason that sailor will go no more a-roving with the Amsterdam maid is that she gave him a dose of you know what.

Brief respites ashore is one of the things the sea shanties tell us about. "Good morning, ladies all" tells about meeting the girls in port and blowing three years pay in one wild fling. "Can't you Dance the Polka" tells of a seaman spending a whole ninety cents on a girl's dinner only to find out she has another "flash man." The shanties tell us about bad ships, as in "Leave her, Johnny" and betrayal and death at sea in "Lowlands."

I do like the song, "My Last Cigar":
"T'was off the blue Canary Isles, a lovely summer day.
I sat upon the quarterdeck and puffed my cares away.
And as the wisps of smoke arose, like incense in the air,
I sighed because I realized it was my last cigar."
I can just picture that mournful sailor, with a long voyage remaining to South America, having miscalculated or run out of tobacco money, sitting on the quarterdeck with the last puffs of his last cigar. Neither of us smokes. Maybe the song appeals to me because I'm a Quarterdeck myself.

Men have been going to sea for thousands of years. In the old days it was mostly men. Only the captain could take his wife along. It's different on our boat: the captain takes her husband along. Someone has to haul up the anchor, and without benefit of capstan or even a winch.

"Oh blow the man down, ladies, blow the man down,
Way hay, blow the man down.
I'll tell you a story of Ralph on the town,
Give me some time to blow the man down.
Ralph left the harbor to buy him some beer,
Way hay, blow the man down
"Moosehead," he asked. "Mon we don't sell it here,"
Give me some time to blow the man down.
They offered him Pabst, Whisky or Rye,
Way hay, blow the man down.
"It's Moosehead or nothing, I'd rather stay dry."
Give me some time to blow the man down.

For all their romance and the records the tea clippers set, that period in nautical history lasted only about fifty years. They were put out of business by the Suez canal and steam ships. Obsolete. There are only a few tall ships left. Some, like the Cutty Sark, are in museums. But we can all have their sea shanties as souvenirs, to sing and remember.

Chapter 20:

RALPH REEFED

It's always wise to practice using your equipment before you actually need it. Reefing gear, for instance. When we launched 'Dreamer' for the first season it took quite some time to step the mast, puzzle out all the rigging wire, get the boom attached, and so on. The friend who came out to show us how rigging was tuned merely commented that we had roller reefing, but didn't demonstrate how it worked. We were so excited and busy with everything else we just didn't think about it. That was a mistake.

We were an accident waiting to happen.

There's no better way to get in tune with the universe, short of becoming a Buddhist, than to become a boater. A poet might say a sailboat is a metaphor for the universe, but I'm not a poet. An occasional limerick is more my style. I'm not so sure what a metaphor is, some kind of a comparison. A sailboat isn't a comparison that explains the world. It's an example of how the forces of Mother Nature work.

Take speed, for instance. With a car, if you want to go fast, you press on the gas and hope the police aren't watching. In a closed automobile with power steering and brakes, you don't feel the forces of nature. In a sailboat you feel the wind on your face and in your ears. The slightest change in direction is noticeable. You become sensitive to every motion and sound. With your hand on the tiller, you feel the pressure of the water. And no matter how fast you try to make a sailboat go, once the bow wave is the same as the waterline length, it's reached that magic formula dictated by the forces of nature: hull speed. It's not going any faster. Not unless it lifts out of the water and surfs.

As for speed, it may be thrilling for those kids on trapezes to stand on the outside of a sailboat heeled thirty-five degrees. I like to see the boat under me, not look straight down into the water while I hang on with my heart in my mouth.

I like a boat to sail on its bottom, not its ear. With a sailboat, everything has to be in balance, in harmony with Nature. The weight of the keel balances against the pressure of the wind on the sails. Pressing a boat too hard doesn't mean it'll go faster. As the wind blows harder, the boat heels more until a new equilibrium is reached. If it blows too hard, the boat heels too far over. You can't change the amount of keel to achieve a new balance, so you change the amount of sail. That's what reefing is about.

Ralph and I went sailing several times before we had to reef. We were getting pretty confident. It was great-- sunshine, the sound of water gurgling around the rudder. But one afternoon the wind got stronger and stronger until I could hardly hold onto the tiller. Spray was coming over the bow. The boat was trying to tell us something: we were out of balance. The pressure of the wind on the sail area behind the mast was forcing the boat to pivot into the wind. Finally, Ralph and I both had to hang onto the tiller.

"I think we have to reef, Ralph. How do we do that?"

"I guess we'll have to find out."

Ralph slacked off on the main sheet to spill the air out of the sail while he crept up on his hands and knees to the mast to figure out the roller reefing. Of course, the moment we spilled the air the sail started flogging and making an awful racket.

"It's spring loaded," Ralph shouted. "You pull the boom back and roll the sail up on it, then lock it again. I can pull it back, but I can't roll up the sail."

"Let down some of the sail first. You have to let some slack in the main halyard."

All those ropes confused him. "Which one is that?" Finally, he released the main halyard and the end of the boom dropped into the water.

"Don't lower the whole sail, Ralph. Just a couple of feet."

Ralph pulled the sail back up and tried again. He managed to roll up a couple of feet of sail, locked the roller reefing gear back in the gooseneck, and pulled the sail tight. "That's better."

But it wasn't. We weren't overpowered by the wind, but the shape of the sail was all wrong. A main sail is basically a big right triangle. The hypotenuse is the leech and the vertical, the luff, is at the mast. Rolling two feet of luff didn't shorten the leech proportionally. The end of the boom now hung down in the cockpit.

When we tacked it swung across so low we had to duck way down.

"Ouch!" Lucky for Ralph, his head was padded by his Greek fisherman's cap.

"This won't do, Ralph."

Ralph nursed his forehead and studied the sail. "It'll have to be tucked up before it's rolled."

"How are we going to do that?"

"You go up to the mast and release the roller gear," he said. "I'll lift the boom, take in a tuck, and then we can roll the sail together."

"OK," I said, somewhat dubiously, and climbed onto the cabin top. I made a mental note to rig a line from the cockpit to the bow and fix us some safety harnesses so we could clip on. This was not the time to go overboard, not when we could hardly control the boat. I tried to grip the mast with my knees while I figured out the reefing system. I shouted, "Ready!" and looked back at Ralph.

Luckily, he had taken off his cap so it wouldn't blow away. He was standing in the cockpit with his legs straddling the tiller while he tried to lift the boom. Then a gust of wind caught the main sail and flung the boom to the side.

"Ralph!"

Boating is full of sudden surprises. One minute everything is hunky dory and the next all hell breaks loose. First Ralph was suspended between the boom and the boat, his feet hooked on the edge of the coaming and his butt in the water. He tried to pull himself aboard, which tightened the sail. It filled. Then, because no one was minding the tiller, the boat came up into the wind, yanking him aboard. But the jib back-winded and flung us onto the opposite tack. This time Ralph had sense enough to let go of the boom and grab the tiller.

Eventually, we got it sorted out. We took down the main and tried sailing just on the jib, but then we couldn't sail upwind back to the harbor. All we could do was sail back and forth. I didn't want to give it up and motor in. We felt really foolish.

On the second try we reefed the main with a tuck to lift the end of the boom, but then the pressure on the spring-loaded roller reefing just made it unwind again. Defective. It reminded me of buying a used car and not finding out until too late that the parking brake doesn't work.

In the end we took down the jib and sailed back to the harbor under just the mainsail. We got 'Dreamer' tied up safely and collapsed. Our confidence was gone. "We sure botched that," I said.

"Hey, Irma. We didn't break anything. Nobody got hurt, and we learned more about the boat."

"I guess you're right." Now that it was over, it was funny. "I wish I'd had a camera. You were quite a sight with your butt in the water. Buster Keaton couldn't have done it any better."

Ralph tugged at his wet pants. "From now on I'm going to keep a complete set of dry clothes aboard."

"That roller reefing isn't as simple as it sounds."

When we got home we studied reefing systems. The traditional method was time consuming and cumbersome. You had to let down part of the sail, tie up the bottom with little reefing ropes, re-attach the tack and the clew, and raise the sail again. That took too much time. Someone sailing alone when it got that windy would have her hands full. I wanted something simple.

Later, on a day when there was no wind, we raised the main and marked it for two lines of reef points, each reducing the sail area by about twenty percent.

Ralph ordered sailmaking supplies from Goldstein's marine-- a sailmaker's palm, needles, thread, some Dacron cloth and four brass cringles.

He made a sketch of the situation. "We've got to make this quick, easy, and safe," he said. "We have to rig a line to keep the boom from drooping, not just that little pigtail that dangles from the backstay."

"You mean a topping lift, Ralph. A rope from the end of the boom to the top of the mast, down, and back to the cockpit."

"Right. Then, if we lead the main halyard back to the cockpit, you won't have to creep up on the cabin top to the mast to let down part of the sail."

"I won't? You mean, you won't, Ralph. But what about the roller reefing?"

"No good. Let's go to slab reefing." He showed me how a single line could be run from the boom up through a cringle in the leech, down to a block, forward along the boom to another block, up to a cringle in the luff, down to the gooseneck, and back to a cleat on the boom. It sounds complicated, but it's really very simple.

Ralph brought the mainsail home and sat in front of the TV surrounded by sail cloth while he sewed diamond-shaped reinforcement patches for reef points. He reinforced the luff and leech for the cringles.

"You look quite a sight, surrounded by all that sail," I told him. "Like an old salt."

"This is easy. Imagine sitting in the foc's'le of a clipper ship struggling to repair the seams in a thousand square feet of heavy canvas."

"There's just one thing missing."

He peered at me over the top of his reading glasses. "What's that, Irma? An eye patch and peg leg?"

"You should be wearing your cap." I put it on him. "That's better." He looked so cute. "When you're done with the sail, I have some wool socks you can darn."

Now reefing is a routine either of us can do single handed. First, the main sheet is eased. Then the topping lift is taken up, lifting the end of the boom. The main halyard, which I marked with colored yarn for the first and second reef, is slacked off. Then haul on the single reefing line to pull the sail tight at the new tack and clew. The pocket of sail can be gathered up neatly by tying the reefing points or, in an emergency, just left for the time being. No more Ralph hanging overboard getting a wet behind, and no need to creep along the cabin top to the mast.

Once reefed, the boat is in balance with nature again. You feel the wind in your ears. The wind on the sails makes the boat heel until the keel balances it. The hull finds its rhythm with the waves. You set the sails so they pull just right, and feel the gentle tug of a balanced tiller.

Ralph feels a kinship with the old sailors of the clipper ship days. He idolizes iron men on wooden ships. He is awed by their courage to climb tall masts and haul in topsails in an Atlantic sleet storm. That's not for me. What I like best about boating is that sense of harmony with the universe.

Chapter 21

WEATHER WATCHERS

Ralph and I were lounging in the cockpit of 'Dreamer' while Oscar the autopilot steered. "This is the life," Ralph said. "I wish my truck could do this-- drive itself while I take it easy. Look at those clouds."

Ralph was laid back against the coaming in his Moosehead beer Tee shirt, with his Greek fisherman's hat covering his receding hairline. Zinc oxide protected his nose and lips from the sun. His wrap-around girl-watching sunglasses shielded him from ultra-violet. He had smeared sun screen on his arms and his bare feet. Tanning is no longer chic.

Ralph has learned his lesson about sunburn and wears white cotton slacks to cover his legs. His knees were never that attractive anyway.

Ralph pointed with his bottle of beer. "That cloud looks like your mother. See the nose?"

We had a brisk southwest wind and weren't sailing anywhere in particular. The clouds Ralph was referring to were scudding along at quite a pace. The waves on the bay were building slowly, giving 'Dreamer' an easy motion that sometimes flung a mist of spray over the bow.

"There are two layers of clouds, Ralph," I said. "Moving in different directions. The upper layer is coming in from the west."

"Remember Peter Heaton's old book on cruising? He had all those sayings about the weather, like 'Red sky at dawning, sailor take warning.'"

"Funny how they made up those."

"That was BTV," Ralph said. "Before television. Sailors had long periods with nothing to do but watch the water, the sky, and the stars. Think how many millions of years humans have been watching clouds. No wonder the Tahitians figured out how to navigate by stars and wave patterns. Look at what we're in now: two sets of waves, an old set coming from the east and this new one from the south west."

At that moment 'Dreamer' hit a bigger swell and water sluiced back over the cabin top. "Getting a little rough," Ralph said, and closed the cabin slide. "That must have been a freak wave, the combination of the south west wave pattern plus one from the east."

I remembered one of those weather sayings, "Mackerel sky and mare's tales make tall ships carry low sails."

"Mare's tails are high, wispy cirrus clouds, first sign of a cold front," Ralph said. "But what's a mackerel sky?"

I described a layer of clouds patterned like fish scales. A mackerel has stripes.

"No mackerel sky today," Ralph said. "But I don't like the looks of that."

The old saying is that everybody talks about the weather but nobody does anything about it. That's not exactly true. People may not change the weather, but they prepare themselves for it.

To the west, the high layer of thin overcast was darkening into an ominous bank. The south wind we had taken on the starboard beam was backing. "Time to change course," I said, and disconnected the autopilot. "We better head back. That's a cold front."

"I think we should take in a reef, just in case," Ralph said. "Head her up into the wind."

Thanks to bad past experience and Ralph's tinkering, we now have a slick jiffy reefing system. In six quick steps he had the mainsail reefed: First slack off the main sheet to take the pressure of the wind off the sail. Second, take up the topping lift to lift the end of the boom. Third, slack off the main halyard to a place marked with colored yarn. Fourth, haul in on the single reefing line. Then he released the topping lift and re-set the main. 'Dreamer' was a little slower, but no longer pressed by the freshening breeze.

"Very neat," I said, "You're getting to be an old pro."

Ralph slipped into the cabin and turned on the VHF weather channel. "Rapidly moving cold front," he reported. "Line squalls."

"Now he tells me," I said. "Why didn't you check the weather report before we left?"

"It was nice before we left."

When I was a girl, before televised weather satellite pictures, the weather person drew a few isobars on a map and stuck in a big L for a low or an H for a high. Now you can actually see the cloud formations and track the progress of a hurricane, even pick out its eye. The TV weather show has cute graphics, little flashing lightning bolts, and undulating broad lines for the jet stream.

What they told us in our boating safety course was that low pressure systems move like waves rolling in on the shore. They gradually build up, taking the shape of a breaking crest. The winds blow toward the center of the low, first from the east, then backing counter clockwise. When the front passes, the wind shifts to the northwest or west. How hard the wind blows depends on how deep the low is, and how fast it's moving. Generally, the harder it blows, the sooner it passes, but a really big depression can go on for several days, and the gusty winds that follow it aren't conducive to lazy sailing. "It's going to get nasty, Ralph. Let's go back," I said.

We were several miles from the marina. The wind that had forced us to reef suddenly died. The bank of dark clouds was high and ominous. Ralph started looking for the sack of foul weather gear. He stuck his head out of the cabin to hand me my storm suit. The clouds glowed briefly, followed by a rumble of thunder.

At the next flash, I counted. A thousand one, a thousand two, and so on. Then the thunder. I had counted to ten. Sound travels about eleven hundred feet a second, or about a mile in five seconds. "It's only two miles away, Ralph. We better batten down the hatches."

Ralph was animated. He danced into his high storm pants. "If the front's moving at twenty miles an hour, we've got about six minutes. What'll we do?"

"It's going to blow. We're too far from the harbor to run for it and too deep to anchor. Let's take down the main and heave to."

We had practiced heaving to. You take down the main and backwind the jib with the tiller lashed on the opposite side from the jib's set, so the sail is working against the rudder. The boat doesn't stand still, but it doesn't run off, either. The effect is a slow forward motion. The motion of the boat will be dampened as long as there's a sail up.

There was another flash of lighting, closer this time, and a mighty crash of thunder. "Oh boy, oh boy," Ralph said. "What if we get hit by lightning?"

"Better disconnect the electronics while I lash the mainsail."

Ralph disappeared into the cabin to unplug the radio and depth sounder so a lightning strike wouldn't cook them. I unplugged the autopilot. There was another crash of thunder. The wind had died completely. Now the cloud bank was right over us. It was getting dark.

Ralph stuck his head out. "All set, Irma. We're supposed to be safe from lightning inside a 120 degree cone down from the mast, but I haven't wired the mast step or the shrouds to the keel. If we're hit by lightning, all that electricity is going to have to jump. What'll we do now?"

I opened the lazaret hatch. "We have to give the lightning a path to follow into the water."

"Yeh, Irma, and not through us."

"Let's hang the anchor by its chain from the backstay. See if you can find a big shackle."

Now we could see a gray line that obscured the shore. We were really in for it. I hung the anchor in the water and Ralph screwed a shackle through a link of the chain and the rigging wire. "There!" he said.

"I'll get the weather boards."

Now everything was unnaturally still. Ralph, in his life jacket and storm gear, chewed his lip and looked at the clouds. He had left his girl-watching sunglasses in the cabin.

I laughed. "You are a funny sight, Ralph. That zinc oxide on your nose looks like war paint."

"What's that noise?" He looked up at the mast.

I heard it, too. It sounded like the buzz of a neon   sign.

"It sounds like electricity," Ralph said. "Maybe we'll see St. Elmo's fire."

I had read about balls of electrical energy glowing up and down the mast. "I don't think I want to see St. Elmo's fire. Not on our boat."

There was another flash of lighting and an almost immediate crash of thunder. Without another word, Ralph hopped over the weather boards into the cabin and closed the hatch.

"Don't touch anything metal," I said. "Stay away from the chain plates." We both peered out the portholes and watched. A line of spray from the rain approached like a tidal bore.

"Here it comes, Irma!" The storm hit very suddenly, filling the jib and heeling 'Dreamer' way over. The rain sluiced over the windows like a fire hose. The noise was terrific. The bow swung downwind. I couldn't see into the cockpit because of the weather boards, but was glad the cockpit is self-bailing.

"How about a hug?" Ralph said.

We sat, holding each other and saying a little prayer.

Like the old seaman's saying, "Long foretold, long last; Short notice, soon past." In fifteen minutes the squall was over. As the rain slacked off to a few sprinkles, Ralph and I emerged from the cabin. Everything was OK. Nothing was damaged, though a corner of the mainsail had blown out of its lashings. We took the anchor back aboard and sailed home.

Afterwards, I told Ralph, "You were quite a sight there in the cockpit. I haven't seen anything like that since 'The Little Rascals,' on TV. Remember how the kids' hair stood on end?"

"I was scared, all right. Did my hair really stand on end?"

"Straight up, Ralph. Must have been that static electricity."

Ralph gave me a weak smile. "Weren't you scared?"

"Plenty."

"Imagine what Cape Horn must be like?"

"Terrifying, Ralph. We'll leave Cape Horn to Slocum. Next time before we go out we listen to the weather report."

"But we did OK, Irma. You just have to know what to do and be prepared. That was a good idea about the anchor as a temporary ground plate."

"Yes. Now tell me how we fix an electrical bond between the mast step, the chain plates, and the keel. That'll be our next weekend project."

Chapter 22

PAN! PAN! PAN!

Before we bought 'Dreamer' the only radios we had were AM/FM receivers. Back during the CB fad Ralph thought about buying one of those for his pickup. He found a copy of the ten code someplace. That's a code worked out by someone who knew the first word of a transmission was often garbled. The word "Ten" was a throw-away. "Ten-four" means "I understand your message. What's your twenty?" means "Where are you?" and stuff like that.

Ralph tried to learn it, in preparation for buying a CB. I'd ask him to wash the dishes and he'd say, "Ten-four." He said every trucker had a 'handle.' He thought about calling himself 'Moosehead' so he could talk to good buddy truckers who had their 'pedal to the metal' in convoys evading Smoky the Bear highway patrolmen.

I dissuaded him. "They'd probably call you 'Meathead,' not 'Moosehead.'" Ralph didn't have a snappy reply that wouldn't precipitate the wrath of some beefy driver of an eighteen wheeler.

He thought about having a CB on a boat. Some fishermen use it, but the range is only about five miles. Ralph suggested, "CB would be OK if I was in the truck and you were on the boat at the marina. You could catch me on the way to the grocery store."

"If you were going to the grocery store, you'd have a list," I told him.

Then came VHF. 'Dreamer' came with a VHF marine band FM transceiver. Suddenly we were radio communicators, or were about to be. In our Coast Guard Auxiliary boating safety class they had talked about marine radio. We needed a license for our ship to shore radio from the FCC, the same government agency that oversees television stations and short wave radio hams. We also needed individual radio telephone operator's licenses.

It turned out to be pretty simple. We could get our individual radio telephone permits free. The application procedure was primarily a screening device, limiting the users to US citizens. No foreign agents or Mata Haris need apply. But we also swore that we had read and were familiar with the federal regulations. That was not so simple.

The application for a new, five-year station license for 'Dreamer' was also free, but the law requires that a copy of the regulations be kept on board, and a log maintained of all radio contacts. So though we got our licenses for nothing, we had to subscribe to the FCC Marine Rules and Regulations and keep them on board and up to date.

I put them in a loose leaf binder. Changes and updates kept coming in, with you-know-who in charge of posting the changes. "You're such a whiz at office records," Ralph said, putting on his sweet face.

"I may have to post the updates," I told him, "but you're supposed to read them, too."

"Sanding old bottom paint is more fun than reading all that fine print," Ralph complained.

In due time we received our station license, with our own call sign, WRV-7858. Ralph made a nice frame for it to put up in 'Dreamer's cabin, as the law requires.

We are supposed to keep that radio on all the time on channel 16, the calling channel, in case someone has an emergency message. We kept the radio on the first few times we went out aboard 'Dreamer' but the air was full of chit-chat. I didn't care if the 'Bottoms Up' was out of beer, or if the cards aboard the 'Busted Flush' had blown overboard. Besides, since we have only outboard power and no solar recharger, keeping the radio on all the time ran down our battery.

The reason we went sailing was to get away from it all, not join a huge party line. If we wanted to do that we could tune our radio direction finder to the wave lengths used by wireless telephones. We don't listen in to private conversations or peep through keyholes, either.

We sort of forgot about sending messages. Then we got caught in the fog.

Life on the water changes rapidly. We started out on a lazy afternoon. One minute the sun was shining. The next, the horizon was obscured by something gray. Then we were in it. Fog. The temperature dropped about twenty degrees. We put on our sweaters. 'Dreamer' was covered with tiny drops of water. We could hardly see the bow. It was as if we had been transported to the Twilight Zone.

Ralph ducked into the cabin. "I better mark our position on the chart before I forget where we are. What's our course?"

The sails had hardly been drawing. Now they hung slack. "Becalmed," I said.

"You should blow the fog horn," Ralph said, and came up with our brass trumpet. "Once a minute."

I blew: Mooooo. "Somebody will think a cow is out taking a swim."

"Watch out for bulls," Ralph said.

At that moment there was a tremendous blast of a ship's fog horn.

I nearly jumped out of my skin. Ralph laughed. "You must have blown the mating call."

"Maybe you should announce us on the radio," I suggested.

"How do I do that?"

"Turn to the proper channel, squeeze the microphone button, and call."

As if to goad him into action, the ship's horn blasted again. It was coming closer.

I blew back a pitiful "Moooo" convinced that nobody six stories up on the bridge of a real ship could possibly hear it.

Ralph asked, "What channel do ships use?"

"I don't know. Look it up. It's on a card."

Ralph found it on the shelf with the regulations. "There's inter-ship safety on six, but there are notations for freighters on ten and twelve. I'll try six." Ralph squeezed the microphone and shouted, "This is 'Dreamer'. We can't see you, can you see us?"

No reply.

"You have to take your hand off the button or you can't receive," I said.

"Oh." He tried again. Still no answer. "I hope they can see our radar reflector."

We have this teeny radar reflector Ralph bought from Goldstein's Marine. We run it up on the port flag halyard. Finding its reflected return on a radar screen must be like looking for a fly speck in a sea of coffee grounds.

The ship's fog horn blasted again. I wasn't sure of the direction. "We better start the outboard, Ralph. Just in case we have to power out of the way." I pulled on the starter rope and, after a couple of tries, got it going.

"Maybe they're not listening to six. We're supposed to call first on channel sixteen, then switch." Ralph changed to the calling channel. "What am I supposed to call? Mayday?"

"Save that for the moment before we're run down. Mayday is only for life-threatening emergencies, like when we're sinking."

I strained my eyes at the fog, expecting at any moment to see the huge, steel bows of a ship bearing down on us. I couldn't see a thing. "Try 'Pan! Pan! Pan" That's for an urgent message."

Ralph called again. "Pan pan pan! 'Dreamer' calling. We hear your fog horn, but we can't see you. Can you see us on your radar?"

"Better say 'over' so he knows it's his turn to talk."

Ralph did that.

A strong voice came over the radio. "You're OK skipper. Just hold your course. We'll pass about a hundred yards to your east."

The next blast was even closer. Can you imagine being run down by a huge ship? One big crunch. Anything still alive gets macerated in the propellers. We heard the engines, and heaved wildly on a bow wave. Then we heard the screws, swish-swishing, but we never saw the ship.

When the ship had passed safely, Ralph let out a long breath. Then he pulled his Greek fisherman's cap down on his forehead. "He called me 'Skipper.'"

"You better thank him," I said and shut off the outboard.

"Gee, yeh." Ralph returned to the radio. "Thank you, captain," he said. There was still a quaver of fear in his voice. "This is 'Dreamer' WRV-7848. Signing off."

To our surprise, the other ship answered. "Old Milwaukee. Have a nice day, sir."

"Gee, he called me, sir."

"If your ego lights up any more than this, Ralph, you'll be calling every ship within range."

"Old Milwaukee! Do you think that was a beer boat?"

"We'll never catch him now, Ralph. Not with our outboard."

"Maybe the Moosehead brewers have their own ship, too."

"Better concentrate on our radio log, Ralph. Enter the time of the transmission, the ship called, and so on." I blew the fog horn again. Moooo. "This could get pretty tiresome. I hope the fog clears soon."

"Our first radio contact," Ralph said proudly.

"At least you didn't yell 'Mayday.' They'd have sent the Coast Guard after us."

"I suppose so. He didn't say 'over'."

"He's not an old pro like you, Ralph. You could have asked him our position. Did you figure out where we are?"

"I forgot."

"Well, check the chart and write down the time. Oh, and leave the radio on channel sixteen. Somebody may be wanting to call us."

Chapter 23

LOST

At dawn I knew something was wrong. We knew where we were at sunset-- more or less--but during the night Ralph and I got scared by a line squall. We were so busy changing headsails and reefing in the dark and the pouring rain that we didn't think much about updating our dead reckoning position on the chart.

'Dreamer' is too small to have a chart table and navigation station like bigger boats. The chart was spread on the dinette table. To protect charts from spilled coffee and peanut butter, Ralph hinged a permanent sheet of plastic window material to the dinette. The chart slips under it, and we use an erasable felt tip pen to mark our position on the plastic. That works OK, but somehow, during all the shemozzle, some rain got on the plastic and we lost our position.

After the squall I went below for some sleep. When Ralph woke me up for the pre-dawn watch, there wasn't a star in the sky. No moon. The night was so dark that I couldn't tell up from down. That was weird, like sailing through the blackness of outer space. I got so disorientated that I kept checking my lifeline to make sure I was clipped on to the boat for fear of falling overboard. Like a couple of kids in a fairy tale, Ralph and I might have been sailing off to Never-Never Land.

The only lights were the compass and Sumlog, glowing a reassuring red. If I hung over the transom I could see the faint glow of our stern light. But I didn't want to hang over the transom for fear of losing my balance.

When early dawn finally brought a glow in the overcast, it was clear enough which direction was up. Looking down, I was actually relieved that we were still on the water. The sails were drawing nicely and we were making an easy four knots, direction 330 degrees. But there was no horizon, just haze.

Ralph stuck his head out of the cabin. "Any idea where we are?"

"East of the Sun and West of the Moon."

"Maybe it's time we learned how to use our radio direction finder."

Ralph bought our RDF as a close-out bargain, but aside from lining it up with the direction of the boat and fiddling with the rotating antenna, we hadn't practiced. I knew the theory, and we had the manual.

According to the manual, the RDF principal was that the Coast Guard has groups of four or five transmitters that send a coded signal all on the same wave length. Each station sends its signal for one minute, like dot-dash-dash, followed by a long tone you can home in on to take a bearing. Then the next station broadcasts, and you take down the next bearing, and so on. Mark the bearings on your chart to the location of the transmitters and where the lines cross, presto, that's where you are. Simple, right?

What the manual that came with that close-out bargain RDF was that the system is obsolete and the Coast Guard no longer broadcasts those signals. We clicked on the Marine band, but we couldn't hear anything. No RDF transmitters. So much for Ralph's bargain deal.

The only option left was to home in on the antenna of an AM radio station. But where was one and would it show on our chart?

Finally we got one on the AM band, a dinky station WPOR broadcasting from a hamlet called Grand Portage. There's a harbor there. "I found the signal for WPOR," I said, "but getting a null is pretty soppy." The best I could do was five degrees plus or minus. But where was the tower? In the town, on a high hill outside?

I got one other AM radio sttion signal, and that was almost 180 degrees in the other direction. The result was that we were somewhere in a long band. I wasn't happy with the faint third bearing. It put us only in a general area. We could be several miles in any direction.

The error could be my fault. The time to practice not being lost was when we weren't lost yet. I re-read the little manual and saw that the signal was not only no more accurate than five degrees, but that land masses could distort it. "An RDF is not an exact instrument, Ralph," I said with some frustration. "Now I know why Goldstein's Marine put these on a close-out sale."

"If we had GPS we'd know exactly where we are."

"We don't have a GPS, Ralph."

"I was just hinting, Pussycat. Christmas is coming. Only five shopping months left."

Ralph hadn't brushed his hair and tufts stuck up. He wiped the water marks off his reading glasses. The light reflected on the lenses made him look like a surprised owl.

I quoted Edward Lear, "The Owl and the Pussycat went to sea in a beautiful, pea green boat."

"I hope they brought the light lists."

We don't have a whole copy of the annual light lists. Our university library has it and I make xerographic copies of the pages for our sailing area. We keep them in a notebook along with navigation and distance off tables out of Bowditch. "They're only useful if you can see lights."

"Any buoys?" Ralph got out the binoculars and swept the horizon-- or rather, where the horizon should be if it were visible.

"Not a thing. Why don't you make some tea? I'm cold."

Ralph came out and stretched his back. "I'll take over. The water's heating on the stove."

With cups of tea sweetened with honey we studied the log and tried to reconstruct our position from the night before. I had entered our estimated position in the log book, and after the squall we had kept a course of 330 degrees.

Our mechanical Sumlog came with the boat and is obsolete, too. It has a little propeller under the boat. Like the speedometer on a car, it has an odometer, but it only measures distance traveled through the water at speeds over a knot. And it isn't entirely accurate because of friction in the cable. It reads low.

Of course, if you are moving with or against a current, it won't tell you the speed over land.

I subtracted the Sumlog reading we had logged the night before from what showed on the dial. We had gone twenty-two miles. Or was that really twenty five? And how much current might have thrown us off?

"How deep is the water, Ralph? Maybe we can get a line of readings off the depth sounder and find it on the chart."

Ralph turned on the depth sounder. He announced, "No bottom."

First a night with no up or down, now a sea with no bottom.

Our depth sounder is only good to three hundred feet, and that's where the bottom is hard. Ooze won't bounce a sonar signal the way rock does. "At least we won't run aground. Let's sail west until we get a reading." We could have been navigating along the fifty fathom line on the chart, but the sounder isn't reliable at that depth.

Ralph was worried. "If I had learned to use the sextant I could shoot the sun."

"Not in this overcast, Ralph."

"What would the Vikings do?"

"Sail west until they hit the coast, then north or south until they spotted something familiar."

It's a scary feeling, being lost on the water. The coast we were sailing along was pretty featureless. No high mountains, no skerries, no prominent islands. At least the RDF bearings on a couple of AM radio towers put us in a general area. The bottom sloped gradually, so using the depth sounder we weren't likely to be surprised by a submerged rocky shelf with deep water right up to its edge.

We had enough experience to know that islands distinct on the chart merge with each other on the horizon, so you can easily miss the entrance to a cove. Small harbors are visible only when you are close, and if they are well marked.

"The depth sounder shows bottom," Ralph announced happily. The nearest land was straight down.

We marked a slip of paper with the distance scale off the chart and took a line of depth soundings, marking a depth at each half mile of distance traveled. Then we lined up the paper with the direction we were sailing on the chart and tried to find the section of the bottom we had passed over. There was no shoreline in sight.

"This could be it," Ralph said. "Not all the numbers for depths marked on the chart coincide, but see this steeper section, like an underwater bluff? I bet we're headed right for Grand Portage. There's a private marina there." We kept the course, had breakfast, and when the haze lifted a little we could see the coast. Gradually features started to show. Distant hills, a few houses, nothing distinctive like a steeple or smoke stack.

Ralph peered through the binoculars. "Aha! A channel marker." He poured over our pages copied from the light lists. "Grand Portage. Didn't I tell you?"

I was suspicious. The little inset on the chart for Grand Portage harbor didn't translate to what I was seeing. "You sure it isn't the Land Where the Bong Tree Grows?"

Ralph imagines he has Viking blood. It's wishful thinking, even if he does have some things in common with Hagar the Horrible. "I shall claim this newly-discovered land in the name of King Olov Red Beard."

"Let's hope the natives don't object."

I spotted a range marker and lined it up carefully. As we cleared the harbor entrance I was sure this wasn't Grand Portage, but who am I to dispute Ralph the Brave, the great Viking explorer?

A cute teen-ager in cut-offs and a Tee shirt stood on the dock. It was obvious that there was no bra under the shirt.

Ah, youth, I thought enviously, putting a new context on Joseph Conrad. Wait till you're forty.

"Need any help?" she called.

"Don't get too excited, Ralph," I muttered. "You'll fall overboard."

We tied up to take a breather from the stress of being lost. "What's Grand Portage like?" Ralph asked the girl.

"Not much of a place in winter. Lots of tourists now. There's a nautical museum if you like that sort of stuff."

There were no tourists in sight, just a few fishing shacks. "Where's the museum?"

"Ten miles down the coast."

Ralph gulped. "This isn't Grand Portage."

"No, this is Petite Portage. Hardly anybody comes here. The harbor entrance is too shallow. The sand bar keeps shifting."

Later, we saw our mistake. The top part Grand Portage harbor mark, seen at a distance, could be mistaken for the whole of the marker at Petite Portage. Lucky for us, 'Dreamer' is a shallow draft boat.

Landing at Petite Portage by mistake taught us a lesson in careful log keeping. Now we practice navigation as if we were lost.

They say that there's nothing quite as memorable as your first landfall after a long ocean crossing. We weren't too far off. It could have been worse. Look at the Pilgrims: Plymouth wasn't their destination. And what about Columbus? He was so relieved at having not sailed off the edge of the earth that he thought he had reached India and called all the natives Indians.

Our next purchase will be a GPS. Then we'll know exactly where we are all the time.

Chapter 24

RALPH'S SECRET STASH

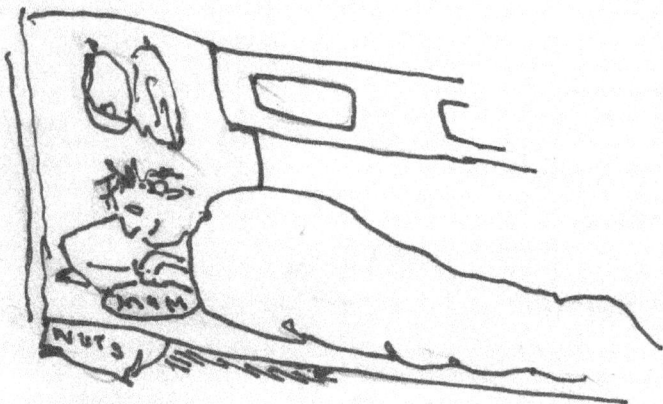

At 23 feet, 'Dreamer' is essentially a weekender. Only the most hardy Spartan could live in that small space for an extended period. Our old pickup camper with its gas/electric fridge and gas stove with oven, not to mention its standing headroom, is luxurious by comparison. But Ralph and I started out as hikers and backpackers, so we're used to roughing it.

'Dreamer' has no hundred gallon water tank and no hot shower. No TV and no electric hair drier. There's also no deep freeze, washing machine, or refrigerator. The list of amenities not aboard is enough to turn off most people who think spending the weekend aboard our 'yacht' is akin to a Princess cruise. The limitations also made planning for a cruise a new experience for us.

When we were backpackers Ralph and I had a tiny gasoline stove and canteens, but I hadn't done meals on a single burner in a long time. And I hadn't cooked on an alcohol stove. There's a big difference between the heat produced by our old gasoline back-packing stove, which was essentially a full force blow torch on end, and the controllable propane burners in the camper. Alcohol stoves like the one we have on our boat are supposed to be the safest--the only fuel that can be put out by smothering it with a wet rag, but the flame is invisible, and cooking a big pot of soup seems to take forever. I was going to have to adjust my menus.

I told myself, "Heck, Irma, you're only going on a week's cruise. It's not an expedition to the South Pole." I'd read a lot about provisioning for long voyages at sea, how people label all their canned goods with indelible ink and then remove the paper labels--in that order, not the reverse--so water in the bilge doesn't take the labels off, clog the pumps, and make the opening of each can of food a great mystery adventure. "What's inside? Beans or peaches? What? Stew for breakfast again?"

Someone even published an article on how to read the packing codes stamped in the bottoms of the cans so if the labels and the marks did wash off, it would still be possible to decipher something. Some long distance voyagers painstakingly varnish the cans so they are less likely to rust while knocking around for months in a damp locker.

Ralph and I weren't going out for several months, or even several weeks. If Ralph and a couple of his buddies went on a cruise, I suppose they'd take cans of beans, lots of beer, instant coffee, bread, and pretzels. The idea of beans three meals a day doesn't appeal to me.

There's a big difference between throwing some things in the cooler, with or without a lump of ice, for an overnight, and going off for a week. For starters, our ice box is just that. It takes ice. Put in more than ten pounds, and there's no room left for food. It's not insulated with the prescribed minimum of three inches of foam. Our ice melts overnight, and then things like fresh fish or meat will spoil. Lettuce will rot, cheese go moldy. What might lay in the back of the fridge at home for a week or two before turning into something ghastly, green, and growing could attack in only a few days aboard 'Dreamer'.

I knew eggs would keep. Fresh eggs can keep without refrigeration for up to six weeks. Boiled and shelled, they can be kept in a jar of vinegar for months. But thanks to Ralph's cholesterol we don't eat many eggs.

We had to make sure our food was nutritious, tasty, and safe. Food poisoning is dangerous at any time. An attack of diarrhea aboard 'Dreamer' would be a nightmare. The portable toilet that came with our boat is one of those dumb things with over four gallons of flush water in the top part, but only three gallons in the holding tank at the bottom where it counts. A two gallon flush tank would have made more sense. We can always refill that with a bucket. Didn't the designers realize that we were going to put something in the bottom tank besides just flush water? Somewhere along the line we'd have to dump the holding tank-- and not overboard.

"Maybe we could bury the stuff ashore," Ralph suggested. "I've already got a canoe paddle aboard. Maybe I should stow an Army surplus entrenching tool."

"People will think you're planning a garden, Ralph."

"I could say we were after buried treasure."

After that remark we named the toilet holding tank the treasure chest and in public places make cryptic remarks about buried treasure.

Planning for a week aboard was a whole lesson in ecology. Besides human waste, there's garbage. Like all good Americans, in a week Ralph and I fill at least three garbage cans. When the kids were at home it could be five or six. I had to plan provisions that produced minimum garbage. No glass gallon jugs. I would transfer items like breakfast cereal to plastic containers that could nest when empty. Plastic bags would have to tightly seal any awful offal until we found a Dumpster.

I'd read about sterilized milk that keeps without refrigeration until opened, but couldn't find any. Powdered milk mixed when we needed it would eliminate bulky plastic jugs of fresh milk that not only require refrigeration but also have to be disposed of when empty.

A week meant 21 meals, plus coffee breaks.

"You have to respect this menu," I told Ralph. "No sneaking snacks or raiding the larder. If you drink all your beer the first day, that's your headache. But if you fix a midnight sandwich, don't eat the pickles I've laid on for Thursday."

"Gee, Irma," Ralph complained. "This is supposed to be a vacation, not the army."

"This is the navy, Ralph, and I run a tight ship."

Ralph studied the menu. "This would be simpler if we caught fish, dug clams, and used seaweed for the vegetables."

"It's hard to schedule a catch, Ralph. Can you catch me a tuna for sandwiches on Wednesday?"

"I might be able to snare a sea gull."

"What is this, Ralph? Survival at sea week?"

"I'm beginning to think so." Faced with that rigid menu plan, Ralph pulled a long face. "A least add a big jar of peanut butter in case we get marooned someplace. Or delayed." He didn't say anything more.

We packed up everything and set off.

The first day, before the ice melted, we had a nice salad. Non-perishable vinegar and oil dressing. The night was glorious. We anchored in a sheltered cove and sat in the cockpit until past midnight. For once, we were far from the light pollution of the city.

"When have we seen so many stars?" I asked.

"On our honeymoon. Remember that little tent? And the mountains? There were shooting stars that night."

I remembered. "And a stick under the tent. It dug a groove in my back."

"That was the second night," Ralph corrected.

We both sat silent, remembering.

Ralph put his arm around me. "This is like a second honey-moon."

The next morning Ralph was up at first light trying to catch a fish for breakfast. The clouds were lit pink underneath before we could see the sun. It was beautiful.

The ice was gone by the second evening. By the third day the carrots were wilting. That old crunch was gone. I know you can keep carrots on a long voyage by putting them in a sand box, but give me a break, there's just no place aboard a 23 footer to start burying carrots, even if you do have an entrenching tool.

The meals went OK, just. Vegetables out of a can don't measure up to fresh. Chinese bean sprouts from cans have a funny taste. I knew that long voyagers grew their own fresh, green, bean sprouts in jars, but where could I put them even if I was willing to take the trouble?

To be satisfying, food has to be chewed. I was beginning to long for crisp and crunch. I had some low fat corn chips for snacks, but the day after we opened the bag their crunch had gotten a bit rubbery.

I regretted having forgotten to pack a supply of crunchy apples. They store well. But I didn't say anything. After all, I had planned the menu. The rule is, first one who complains cooks. And I was already cooking.

Ralph, bless his heart, didn't say anything. But about the fourth evening when we were sitting under the stars, I heard a peculiar sound. "What was that?"

"Hmmmm?"

"I heard something crunch."

Ralph swallowed. "I didn't hear anything."

There was a rustle of cellophane. I reached into the cabin and brought out the flashlight. "Alright, Ralph, what is it?"

In the beam of my light he looked like a burglar caught in the act. "Ralph, are you snitching food?"

His mouth was full of something. "Who, me? Mess up the menu schedule? No way."

"You're eating something."

Ralph grinned and opened his hand. There was the crumpled wrapper of a snack-sized bag of M&M chocolate candies.

"Chocolate!" I exclaimed. "You skunk. Sneaking chocolate behind my back."

"Hey, Irma, I brought it aboard myself."

"What else have you got?"

He shrugged. "Some peanuts. A few pretzels. Crunchy stuff. I knew the carrots wouldn't last."

"Why didn't you say anything?"

"You're the captain. I didn't want to seem insubordinate."

He wouldn't reveal everything, but I found out he had squirreled away secret stashes all over the boat.

"Got some for me?"

"I might. Depends. What'll you give me?"

"How about a hug?"

"That'll be good for two pretzels."

"What? Only two pretzels?"

He laughed. "Irma, my menu's all figured out. Just so many crunchies for each day. Don't want to upset the fixed, naval routine. I thought you said this was a tight ship!"

Chapter 25

ABOARD THE "SEVEN NO TRUMP"

Cruising can be done from all kinds of boats, from a kayak to a sixty foot yacht. The kayaker doesn't sleep aboard, of course, but goes ashore with her tent. A British couple have sailed in all parts of the world in an open seventeen footer with a boom tent. According to a *Cruising World* magazine survey the average cruising couple lives aboard a 27 footer. That means a forward cabin with a Vee berth often full of sail bags, a tiny head, maybe a quarter berth for the off watch, and a main cabin whose table makes into a bed. Living together in that small space takes discipline and tolerance.

I wonder how some couples do it. Take, for instance, the Trumps. Trump isn't their real name. Like they say in the disclaimer for a movie, "names have been changed to protect the innocent." I'll name them after their boat.

Their boat is the "Seven No Trump." It's a big trawler cruiser built in Taiwan by Leaky-Teaky Ltd. You know the type: lots of hand carving on the woodwork, dragons on the bowsprit, but drips under the skylight.

The "Seven No Trump" tied up in the slip next to ours. It was a hot day and Ralph, dressed in cut off jeans and his favorite Moosehead beer Tee shirt, was bringing a bag of ice from the machine by the marina office when the Trumps arrived.

Compared to ours, their boat is enormous. Mr. Trump, in a white, military-style shirt with epaulets and a blue-billed yachting cap with gold "scrambled eggs," stood on the fly bridge and shouted at his wife on the bow. She stood with a mooring line on the end of a boat hook. Her intention was to drop the loop over a piling while Mr. Trump fiddled with the dual engine controls.

Ralph enjoys watching boaters almost as much as Monday night football and looked on with interest while Mrs. Trump reached with the line. A cross wind caught the "Seven No Trump" and the line missed, falling into the water.

Mr. Trump swore. He's one of those yellers. Mrs. Trump's answering glare could kill at twenty paces. The engines roared in reverse and they made another approach while Mrs. Trump retrieved the line. She made it on the second try.

When she was ready with a docking line, Ralph said, "Throw it here," and caught it with his face. He made a neat figure eight over a cleat, dropping the rest on the dock.

Mrs. Trump was sullen and hardly thanked Ralph, but Mr. Trump was grateful. As soon as he had shut down the engines he opened the gate in the railing of the big trawler and stepped onto the finger pier to flemish down the bow mooring line. He made a nice little flat coil of it. "Why don't you get the stern line?" he told Ralph.

Ralph said, "Yes, sir." As he handed the bag of ice down to me he winked and said, "Here's your ice, Ma'am." Ralph picked up the loose end of one of Trump's lines and asked, "You want that clockwise or counter clockwise?"

"What?"

"Clockwise or counter clockwise?"

Trump was stumped.

"We do ours digitally," Ralph said, pointing to our line. "Sort of back and forth and hanging in the water."

"Oh, you don't work here?" Trump said, embarrassed.

"Nope."

Trump apologized and invited us for a drink at cocktail hour. Before I could refuse, Ralph accepted. I had my doubts about the Trumps.

"Did you notice?" Ralph asked as I put the ice in the cooler.

"Notice what?" I handed him a can of Moosehead Light and opened a diet soda for myself.

"Gloves. She was wearing gloves. For line handling. Probably sold by Land's End with little anchors on the cuffs."

"I bet they don't drink out of cans. They're not our kind of boating people, Ralph. You shouldn't have accepted the invitation."

"Aw shucks, Irma," he said, putting on his Wallace Beery act, "I always wanted to see one of them Taiwanese trawlers on the inside."

I hoped he wouldn't be sorry. I remembered a late night TV re-run. "Just so I don't have to play Tugboat Annie."

By the time the Trumps had hooked up their water hose and thick, yellow shore power cord, the narrow finger pier was an obstacle course that would challenge a tight rope walker. I think he did it on purpose to make things difficult for the guests Mrs. T had invited.

I put on a fresh blouse, but Ralph said it was hot and didn't change. He has a pair of Topsiders, but I think he wore his old Adidas with the holes in the toes just to test the Trumps. Mr. T smiled a welcome, but Mrs. T's eyes saw his shoes at once and she cringed as Ralph stepped onto the teak deck.

"Would you like a tour?" Mr. T asked.

"Sure," Ralph said.

It was actually cold down below. The Trumps were showing off the air conditioning. I could have worn a mink jacket for warmth if I owned one. There was teak everywhere, of course. Curtains matched the upholstery pattern. Sheer luxury. Everything was neat, like they had maid service. Everything except the galley. Someone hadn't bother to wash up and there was a pile of stuff balanced on the narrow counter just waiting for a wake to tumble it off onto the teak and holly floor.

The round bed in the master bedroom was one you could only sleep on in port. At sea you'd roll off in any direction.

"Let me show you the engine room," Mr. Trump said, and launched into a litany of specifications, horsepower, and kilowatts. He had a generator capable of turning the props in an emergency.

Ralph was eager, but I passed up the engine room tour for a soft chair on the open deck. Mrs. T indicated a shaker and built-in liquor cabinet. "Bourbon or a daiquiri?"

I took the daiquiri while she sipped bourbon on the rocks. We had just gotten to the point where I was running out of small talk when a cry announced the arrival of the Trump's weekend guests.

They turned out to be the van Lutens. They both had hard, Samsonite suitcases designed to survive airport baggage handlers, but unstowable on a boat. I could see by the suit Mr. van Luten wore that they were business friends of the Trumps and guessed that Trump was deducting this voyage as a business expense. The cry I had heard was Mrs. van Luten getting her spike heel caught in one of Trump's flemished line booby traps.

Her husband kept her from falling into the harbor and she recovered well enough to make her entrance. "Not those shoes," I said to myself, "not on these teak decks. Not on any deck."

Mrs. van Luten wore a gorgeous two piece green suede outfit. It had to cost hundreds, but I didn't envy her because showing it off in that heat had to be torture.

At that moment, Ralph emerged from the engine room tour. There was a black streak across his Moosehead beer Tee shirt. "Tightened a belt," he explained to me, then saw the van Lutens. "Hi."

Mrs. T handed me her bourbon glass and gave me a cool, commanding look. "Get me some more ice from the galley, honey."

Was I guest or waitress? Things went downhill from there.

Ralph decided to rinse his shirt in the harbor, wrung it out, and draped it over the rail to dry.

Mrs. T tried to get me to wash up her mess in the galley.

Mrs. van Luten spilled a bloody Mary on her green suede slacks and used Ralph's Moosehead beer Tee shirt to wipe it up.

That did it. I had to admire Ralph's ability to control his temper. We excused ourselves and made a quick retreat.

169

Ralph put on another shirt and we walked to town for a hamburger just to distance ourselves from the Seven No Trump.

"I guess there's all kinds of boaters," Ralph said.

"And different ways to treat or be a guest," I told him. "You didn't have to wear those holey shoes or that beer Tee shirt."

Ralph shrugged. "They'll have to sleep with those suitcases. The bed's the only place big enough to stow them." He chuckled. "The only luggage that belongs on a boat is something soft that disappears when empty."

"I bet Mrs. van Luten won't do the washing up. And she looks like the kind who takes long showers. "

"OK as long as they never unhook the shore water hose and stay in port," Ralph said.

To our surprise, that evening Mr. Trump invited himself aboard our boat to apologize. "I'm sorry about the van Lutens," he said. "Business associate. You know how it is. Did you notice those high heeled shoes? She fairly splintered my deck. There's a long scratch in the cabin sole." He moaned and shook his head. "They play good bridge, but they're not boating people like us."

After he left, Ralph looked at me and grinned. "Boating people like us, Irma."

It's become a private joke.

The incident reminded me of something I'd forgotten. We're used to life in small spaces, to brushing our teeth in a cupful of water. But I made a tip sheet for our occasional guests. Besides warning them not to bring any hard luggage, I list:

Something warm for chilly nights,

Waterproof rain gear you can kneel down in in a downpour,

Sample-size plastic bottles of shampoo that stow easily, and won't break into invisible glass splinters in the bilge if they fall down,

A hat that won't blow off,

A supply of plastic bags to separate things that might spill or be damp.

Shoes that won't mar a deck. A fine boat is like a piece of furniture that floats.

For guys like Ralph, I added to the list "Something you could wear in a nice restaurant." A necktie takes up so little space.

Mr. and Mrs. Trump would like that.

Chapter 26

BUGS

It sounded like a World War II dive bomber screaming down over some defenseless English village. I sat up in the bunk so suddenly that I bumped my head. "Damn!"

"What's the matter, Irma?" Ralph asked, aroused from his sleep.

"A mosquito's gotten in the boat. We've got to kill him."

Ralph thought a moment. "Her, Irma. Only the females bite. The female is the most dangerous of most species."

It was a moonless, humid night. Our boat, 'Dreamer', lay at anchor in a quiet gunkhole. We had anchored there because we wanted to watch shore birds in the morning, forgetting that wetlands also mean bugs.

Ralph groped in the dark for the flashlight and snapped it on. He trained the light on the overhead like some searchlight crew during the London blitz. "I don't see anything."

"There's a mosquito in here, Ralph. Believe me." In our tenting days, if we were quick and careful, we could get inside and zip the flap tightly before any bugs got in with us. 'Dreamer's cabin slide was not tight.

"Why don't you just let her bite? She needs some blood or she can't have babies. Baby mosquitoes feed baby fish, and small fish feed the shore birds. Think of your responsibility to the food chain. She'll only bite once, then go off and rest."

"Don't lecture me on biology, Ralph, not at this time of night."

We searched methodically for the mosquito and found it hiding behind a curtain. "Got her!" Ralph said. Now there was a spot of red on the fresh paint. "Too late. She already bit."

"See if there's another one."

We couldn't find any and went back to sleep. Half an hour later, there it was again. Buzz.

We went through the routine again.

The little ventilator hatch over the forepeak was already closed. "I think they're getting in around the cabin slide," Ralph said. "I'll stuff my socks in the cracks. That'll teach them."

"That'll probably attract more."

Finally, with our faces rubbed down with repellant, we tried to sleep. About every half hour another mosquito found its way in. We didn't get bitten, but that didn't keep us safe from fly-overs as the invaders investigated the target area. It was a miserable night.

Finally, Ralph sat up. Like a seal at a breathing hole under the ice, he put his nose up under the mushroom vent installed over the galley. "It's stuffy in here. I've got to get some air. I'm getting claustrophobia." He flung the hatch back and stuck his head out. "No wonder the mosquitoes were fired up. It's raining. Perfect weather if you're a breeding mosquito."

Dawn woke the shore birds. The Acrylan boom tent Ralph sewed last winter as a shelter against the rain and sun made a perfect bird-watching blind. We saw a cormorant, several kinds of ducks, some Canadian geese, a blue heron, and red wing blackbirds. Ralph thought he saw a beaver, but it might have been an otter or a muskrat.

After breakfast we made plans for our defense against bugs.

Ralph suggested those mosquito repellant coils that smolder for about eight hours. Ever since I got a rash from enzyme laundry detergent I always read the fine print on labels. "You can't burn those coils in a space where you sleep, Ralph. We'll get sick."

"We could fumigate the place with flying insect killer."

"Poison, Ralph. Anything that could kill a bug can't be good for us to breathe."

"Then we'll have to make some screens. I've got to have air. I can make a screen in a frame that fits like the weather boards. But it has to be fine enough to keep out no-see-ums. They're smaller than mosquitoes."

I offered to sew a nylon screen for the forward ventilator. They can be held down with fishing weights, elastic, or stuck tight with Velcro strips. Bugs might have gotten in through the mushroom vent, so Ralph put screen under its cover. We completed those projects before we went on another overnight cruise, and, just to be safe, sprayed the repellant around the edges of the cabin slide instead of rubbing it on our own faces. That worked.

We thought we had the bug problem licked. Then we got cockroaches.

Ralph is roachaphobic. He hates cockroaches. In college he and his brother shared an apartment that was infested with them. The cockroach, he says, has been around for hundreds of millions of years and will outlast the humans. That's how smart they are.

Ralph smelled them before he saw them. "Must have come aboard with groceries," he said, poking around under the bunks. "They hide their eggs in corrugated grocery cartons and in the seams of paper bags. Damn. We can sprinkle around the galley and in the corners with boric acid and powdered sugar. They get it on their feet and when they lick it off--curtains! Or make a bait of powdered sugar and plaster of paris. That constipates them to death, but we'll never get them all."

Ralph opened a bottle of Moosehead Lite and eyed the neck suspiciously. He wiped it off with a towel. "They can't open a bottle of beer, but roaches can chew through a plastic bag. They'll eat anything. Shoes, even the starch in book cloth."

"What about roach traps?"

"I'll try anything."

I never saw him so freaked out. At the hardware store he bought a couple of roach hotels. I waited in the cockpit while he installed them. Suddenly there was a yelling and a thumping. "Hey! Gotcha! Take that and... Irma!"

He emerged from the cabin holding up a three inch bug. "What's this?"

"Looks like a cockroach."

"It's a plastic water bug."

I could hardly stop laughing. "Did you kill it?"

"Where'd you get this?"

"At the toy store. Don't throw it out. You can put a fish hook in it and use it as a lure. Or we can take it to a restaurant and slip it on the plate like W.C. Fields and get a free meal."

"It's not funny, Irma."

"Oh, yes it is. You should see yourself."

"Cockroaches aboard ship are not funny."

I have to admit they aren't. Later, Ralph reported that he read in a boating magazine about a man who used wolf spiders to get rid of roaches. Some spiders build webs. Others prowl. Apparently, the wolf spider is a prowler that hunts cockroaches. I've never gotten close enough to a spider to see if its head is shaped like a wolf's, but that's the story.

I asked Ralph where he was going with a couple of peanut butter jars with holes punched in their lids.

"Hunting. I'm after wolf spiders."

"Lots of luck, Ralph. Just make sure you don't get eaten by a black widow."

He was very secretive about the results of his hunt. Just raised his eyebrows and put a finger to the side of his nose when I asked him, as if some roach might overhear our conversation and pass the word.

The next time we went sailing, there was a sign on the weather boards: "Do not disturb resident spiders. They have been hired as 'Dreamer's Roach Patrol." I guess Ralph wasn't afraid the bugs might read.

I took the groceries for our outing below to put them in the locker. It's a dark place. When I reached in with a bag of corn chips I felt something hairy and screamed.

"What's the matter, Irma?"

"There's a rat or something in the locker. It's all hairy."

"Lemme see." He reached carefully into the locker. "Gotcha!" Then he pulled out a gigantic spider and thrust it at my face. "Isn't he cute?"

"Yuck! Take it away."

"This is White Fang. He's only plastic, Irma. But I figure he'll scare the roaches off."

"I'm going to be sick."

"No. He doesn't bite. See?"

I don't know if the cockroaches ever did see White Fang. The boric acid and plaster of paris mixtures seemed to help. I haven't seen any real spiders, not of any size. Ralph drew a picture of a huge spider and printed under it, "Warning: this vessel protected by killer spiders." It won't have any effect on roaches, but it might discourage burglars-- that is, if they can read.

Chapter 27

RALPH AND THE CHINESE WATER TORTURE

"Cabot Cove?" Ralph asked. "Isn't that where the mystery story writer lives in 'Murder She Wrote'?"

"You're mixing up TV with reality again, Ralph. Don't get out your autograph book. Angela Landsbury isn't really here."

Cabot Cove turned out to be a place where we would have to solve a mystery, but it wasn't a murder. Ralph and I had made a long day of it, poking along from Grand Portage over forty miles without much wind. We weren't in a hurry. We got into Cabot Cove on the brief light of a sunset that peeked under the overcast like a golden eye behind a curtain. The last yellow light went out as we tied up at a guest slip. The clouds were heavy, one of those warm fronts that brings steady rain. It was going to be a wet night.

It started to rain while I was making supper. Ralph put up the boom tarp but the cockpit was already wet. Then while he did the dishes I went ashore in just my foul weather gear to take a shower. If we're anchored in some uninhabited gunkhole I can stand in the cockpit in the pouring rain with a bar of soap, but here was civilization. The people in the next boat were the kind who can't walk past a porthole without looking in.

When I got back to 'Dreamer' it was raining hard. I hung up my damp towel on a line under the tarp. The cabin is supposed to be a dry oasis. Did you ever try to put on dry clothes inside foul weather gear? Harry Houdini could wriggle out of a straight jacket, but he never had to change clothes inside of one. I'm not Harry Houdini.

I had to come inside the cabin with my dripping, foul weather gear. At 23 feet 'Dreamer' doesn't have the luxury of a wet locker. Where do you put all the wet stuff? I had to stow it in the forepeak with the sail bags and portable toilet. By that time, the cabin sole was wet.

I sat naked on the bunk and tried to put on my snuggy suit without dragging the cuffs on the wet floor. I didn't want to crawl into the sleeping bag with wet cuffs.

Fortunately, 'Dreamer' is built of fiberglass. How you keep dry on a wooden boat is a mystery to me. In the old days boats were expected to be wet on the inside. Wooden boats have seams that must be caulked. Frames have limber holes built in so the water, especially sweet rainwater, doesn't collect in puddles and start rot. The bilge is expected to be wet. When enough water collects, you pump it out.

I didn't think fiberglass boats like 'Dreamer' had seams. All one piece, right? Wrong. Even a so-called 'Tupperware' boat, built like a plastic refrigerator storage container with a lid, has seams. With all the flexing a boat goes through, something's got to give. Those seams can leak.

Since 'Dreamer' doesn't have an inboard engine with a propeller shaft and weepy stuffing box, the bilge should be dry. It isn't, quite. The hatch for the lazaret doesn't   have a deep enough lip, so when the boat is heeled, some water can trickle in. I also suspect the cockpit drains were sloppily installed.

The first time Ralph found water in the bilge he was frantic. He imagined we would sink immediately. Not only did he pump most of the water out, he soaked up the rest with a sponge and even dried the last dregs with a paper towel. Then he found out that if there was some water in it, the bilge was a cool place for his stash of Moosehead beer. Now it stays wet.

I managed to keep the cuffs of my snuggy suit dry and slid down into the sleeping bag. "Listen to the rain, Ralph," I said.

"Yeh. It reminds me of our honeymoon and the rain on our tent."

There's something soothing and cozy about listening to the rain patter down on the cabin. The gimbaled, kerosene lamp gave off a pleasant, yellow light. I sat up. Something was wrong. "Ralph, my sleeping bag's wet."

"Couldn't be."

"It's wet, Ralph." Aside from the beer bilge, 'Dreamer' is a dry boat, but here was a damp spot. Where did it come from? "My shoulder is wet."

"Lemme see." Ralph wriggled out of his sleeping bag and checked the overhead. Dry. But under the deck behind the curtain it was wet. "Chain plate," Ralph said somewhat cryptically. "It's not coming from the bolts or behind the plate, but where it goes up through the deck. Must be the joint."

"Can you stop it?"

"Not in the rain. Has to be re-bedded."

"What do I do now? The cushion's wet, too."

"It's running down the side. When you lie against it, the sleeping bag acts like a blotter."

We rigged a plastic bag with duct tape to direct the trickle away, and put a towel beside the cushion. It was like lying on a damp sponge. "Why don't we change berths, Ralph? Or is chivalry dead?"

"Sir Walter Raleigh only lay his coat down for the queen to walk on. He didn't offer to sleep in the puddle."

"You could move into the forepeak," I suggested.

"I get claustrophobia in there, Irma. Why don't you move to the forepeak?"

"I don't like to sleep with that portable toilet. It smells."

"Move it in here."

'Dreamer' doesn't have standing headroom. Crouched down in the low cabin Ralph slid the portable toilet out of the forepeak, shifted the sail bags, and got me settled in the vee berth.

By now it was midnight and we hadn't any sleep. Ralph put out the kerosene lamp and we settled down to the pattern of steady rain.

I managed to get comfortable and was almost asleep, but every few moments Ralph would toss and turn. He made funny noises.

"Are you having a nightmare, Ralph?"

He growled and I saw the light of a flashlight.

"I've got one, too," Ralph said.

"A what?"

"A leak."

"Where's it coming from?"

"One of the bolts I put through the cabin top when I installed the topping lift."

Curious, I wriggled out of my bag and knelt by his bunk.

"There," Ralph said, and shone the flashlight on the nut right above his face. While we watched, a drop of water grew on the end of the bolt, heavier and heavier, then dropped. "Argh!"

Another drop began to form immediately. Before it could fall, Ralph soaked it up with a paper towel. "I'll never sleep with this. This is the old Chinese water torture."

"Can't you caulk it?"

"I have a tube of silicone in the tool kit."

I went back to the forepeak but before I turned in I inspected the ventilator hatch. The deck under it was wet. The rain spattered and splashed in. It was either be wet or close it and not have any fresh air.

Ralph lit the kerosene lamp and rummaged around, swearing. Turning a simple bolt is a two person operation. One is outside with a screw driver and the other inside with the pliers. Fortunately, Ralph has a pair of Vice Grip pliers, so he clamped the nut with it while he went in the rain.

I heard him grumbling in the cockpit and thumping on deck. He turned the bolt until the Vice Grip dropped off with the nut. By now his bunk was soaked.

I heard someone shouting outside, "Hey, you! What the hell do you think you're doing?"

I heard Ralph explain, "Got a leak."

The voice asked, "You always fix leaks in the nude?"

"Didn't want to get my pajamas wet."

There was laughter from the next boat and applause.

Ralph came back in the cabin looking sheepish. He pulled on his bathing suit and went back out in the rain. "At least it's a warm night." He smeared the bolt with silicone, put it back in, then made another trip inside to re-thread the nut. Every time he came in he dripped more water.

"You must have been quite a sight, Ralph," I said.

He dried himself with the last towel. "I thought everybody was asleep."

"I'm sorry I missed the show."

"I'll be glad to put one on for you privately, sweetheart." He rolled his eyes. "Anytime." He started to sing "That old black magic" with a grind and bump but hit his   head on the cabin top. "Ouch."

"Some other time, Ralph."

It's not easy to pull your pants on without standing headroom. Ralph sat on the damp bunk to put on his pajamas. "I'm glad the cabin top is solid. If this were a foam core construction, the loads on anything through bolted would compress the core. We'd never keep things tight. If it were balsa cored a leak would eventually cause rot. That would be a mess to repair."

When dawn's early light woke the sea gull chorus I wished 'Dreamer' did have a foam-cored hull. Foam cored hulls are insulated. 'Dreamer' cooled down during the night and every inside surface was covered with condensation. We wiped it down with towels that were already damp.

The rain had stopped. Ralph tackled the chain plate after breakfast, lifting the little trim plate and re-bedding it. I hadn't thought about how much of a load is on the rigging and its points of attachment. Every time the boat rocks, the system pulls, first this side, then that. It's no surprise that eventually it developed a leak.

When Ralph installed the deck fittings for the topping lift the holes he drilled were a little too large, and he forgot to set the bolts in bedding compound. That's why they leaked.

Ralph ran a bead of silicone around one of the windows, a temporary repair that would have to wait until winter lay-up when he could remove the window entirely and set it in new bedding compound.

The leaks were minor but irritating. I remember the days when cabin tops were covered with canvas set in wet paint. A leak in the canvas might travel several feet under it before it found a seam between two planks and entered the cabin.

The story of Ralph's nude escapade spread around the marina by noon. In spite of knowing looks from people in other boats we stayed an extra day in Cabot Cove just to dry out. 'Dreamer' was festooned with our sleeping bags and my snuggy suit hanging out to dry, along with every towel we possessed. The berth cushions lay in the sun all day. I was glad we didn't have a week of rain. After a week we'd look like something in the back of the refrigerator, mold all over our bodies.

Ralph smeared silicone on every place he thought might leak. In the process he discovered some flaws in the hull to deck seam. In stormy conditions, with the bow plunging in the waves, we can expect some leaks there. How we're going to fix that one is the real mystery.

Chapter 28

Hunting the Mail Buoy

Our neighbors, Ted and Gladys are strictly landlubbers. Ted gets nervous if he has to drive through a puddle on the street. Boating's not for them. The only time we got them aboard Dreamer was when we needed their hyperactive son, Toby the Terrible, to ride a bosun's seat to the top of the mast to thread a rope through a block. Gladys claimed she was seasick even though we never left the dock.

Ted and Gladys invited us over for a cookout so Ted could show off his new gas grill. A pot luck. We were bringing desert and our own drinks.

"I thought Gladys was a vegetarian," I said. "You don't do carrot sticks and celery on a gas grill."

Ralph fished a couple of cans of Moosehead Lite out of the fridge. "Don't be surprised if we get tofu hot dogs."

"Blech. Ralph, do we really have to do this?"

"They're our neighbors, Irma. Good neighbors make good neighborhood crime watchers."

Ralph was remembering the time the outboard was stolen and Ted and Gladys didn't notice. Had their blinds drawn.

"The only thing Ted and Gladys ever talk about is their latest toys. Remember their talking ice cream machine?"

"Don't worry," Ralph said. "I'll tell them my old navy jokes."

"You were never in the navy, Ralph."

"My college roommate was. He used to tell about sending some slob in search of midshipman W. T. Door. Guy would go all over the ship looking for W. T. Door. Someone would say they'd seen him up on the bow, or up the crows nest changing a light bulb. Finally he'd get sent down to the bottom of the ship and find the name W. T. Door stenciled on a watertight door."

I'd never heard of a W. T. Door myself and wondered if I'd have bitten on that one.

"Then there's sending someone for a steam blanket, or a piece of shoreline. Shoreline is a sure cure for seasickness. All you need is a yard of it."

It sounded like some kind of rope. "How does it work?" I asked.

Ralph laughed. "You stand on it. Geez, Irma, don't tell me you're that gullible."

"Shoreline. Oh, sure. I get it."

"And there's sending someone for some waterline."

"Uh huh." I couldn't see Ted or Gladys laughing.

"The best one is pulled on young officers," Ralph said. He slipped out of the kitchen and came back wearing his Greek fisherman's cap at a jaunty angle. "They put them on watch for the mail buoy. How else do sailors at sea get any mail from home?"

Wondering which of these tales Ralph was going to pull on Ted and Gladys gave me something more fun to look forward to than tofu hot dogs. I got my no-cholesterol vegetarian whole wheat zucchini bread out of the freezer for our share of the meal and we went next door.

To my relief, I smelled real meat. Ted had mercifully taken the plunge and bought steaks for the christening of the grill.

We dutifully stood by in admiration while Ted, in his chef's hat and "I'm the cook" apron, explained all the intricacies of their new gas grill. It had a side burner for a coffee pot, a window, neat shelves where Ted had lined up an assortment of sauces, and a row of utensils-- forks, spatulas, skewers and knives that reminded me of a surgeon's operating room.

Toby the Terrible seized a large butcher knife, said "What's this for, Dad?" and made off with it like the villain in some slasher film.

Ted kept the kid at a distance with a long-handled Bar-B-Q fork. "Toby! Put that down!"

Toby pointed the knife at his father. "Hey, Zorro!"

Ralph took Toby firmly by the wrist and the back of his neck and removed the butcher knife. "Easy there master Jim 'awkins," Ralph said in his Wallace Beery voice. "There'll be no mutiny aboard this ship."

There actually were tofu hotdogs, but only Gladys was eating them.

We settled down to steaks charred on the outside with the middle a bit too rare for me.

Ted caught my hesitation. "Haven't quite got the hang of it."

"You will," I said. "Tastes fine."

Gladys merely commented, "Meat will ruin your colon. It just lays in your guts and putrefies."

Ted changed the subject. "Been out on your boat lately?"

"Yes," Ralph said, beaming. "Saw something astonishing."

"What's that? Catch a funny fish?"

"Nope." Ralph put down his can of Moosehead. "Saw a phone buoy."

"A phone buoy?"

"You know how MCI and Sprint are trying to compete with AT&T. Now they've come up with a new service for boaters. Floating telephone booths."

"I thought everybody had radiotelephones."

"Oh, no. You don't want a telephone on your boat, Ted. People go boating to get away from the office and all the hassle. If you have a phone on your boat you're never free of it."

"Then who needs a phone buoy?"

"To call home. To tell your mother you're all right. Or maybe to tell the boss that you're broken down on the freeway and can't get to the office."

Ted swallowed, nodded, and reached for the ketchup. "Makes sense. Do they anchor these phone buoys in the harbor?"

"Some," Ralph said. "But where the water's too deep, they just drift around."

Ted was puzzled. "Seems kind of dumb to me. If phone buoys just drift around, how do you ever find them?"

"They put out a signal you can home in on with a radio direction finder," Ralph said, warming to his task. "They send a dot and a dash. That's Morse code for E. T. Get it?"

Ted didn't, but Toby the Terrible did. "I get it, Dad. E. T. Phone home! Pretty neat."

Ralph patted Toby on the head. "Smart boy." The kid hates being patted on the head.

Ralph continued. "They also send out their current latitude and longitude so people with LORAN can just enter the location as a waypoint and are guided right to them."

"Sounds a bit complicated to me," Ted said. "You boaters and your electronics. How does a phone buoy get the power to do all that?"

Ralph gave me a sidelong look and grinned. "Just like a space satellite-- solar panels."

Even with mustard, relish, and chopped onion Gladys had not finished her tofu hot dog. "That's amazing. What do these things look like?"

"A British phone booth," Ralph said, "with solar panels on the roof, dingly rods to discourage sea gulls from pooping on the panels, and an antenna with a strobe light. There's also a cleat so you can tie your boat to it while you make a call."

"That's great," Ted said. "I wonder why Ma Bell didn't do that years ago."

"Competition is the soul of capitalism," Ralph said. "Just to make sure you're signed up, the phone buoy doesn't take change. You have to use your AT&T calling card."

Ted shrugged. "Lucky we aren't boaters, Gladys. We switched to MCI."

It was my turn. "They've also added WC buoys."

Gladys didn't understand. "WC?"

"Public toilet buoys. To cut down pollution. You know how endangered the waterways are, what with fishermen like Ralph relieving themselves over the side. There's a new coast guard regulation. No dumping effluent overboard. People in small boats without toilet facilities like our open fishing boat-- the one we sold when we bought Dreamer-- no longer have to suffer. There are now WC buoys being placed in popular fishing areas."

Toby piped up. "And at the beach so people won't pee in the ocean?"

"Right," I said.

"Gee, Irma," Ralph said. "I didn't read about that."

There was a gullibility all over his face. "You didn't? You better watch out, Ralph. If you don't use the WC buoy you might get a ticket from the coast guard." I couldn't keep a straight face any longer and laughed.

Gladys laughed, too. "A toilet buoy? Ralph, you didn't believe that!"

Toby jumped up from his seat and ran around the picnic table to thump Ralph on the head. "E. T. Phone Home! E. T. phone home!"

We all cracked up. Ralph looked so sheepish.

Ted thought it was great. "Phone buoys. WC buoys. What a joke! You people are wonderful neighbors. Never a dull moment."

Chapter 29

A PLACE FOR EVERYTHING

I was talking one day to one of those cute college boys who has a summer job at the marina. He was mystified. Why, he asked, would anyone invest a fortune on a boat so they could spend a vacation crouched in a space smaller than a cheap motel room with no TV and no hot shower. I told him that you don't have to invest a fortune to become a yachtie. Our 23 foot boat, bought used, cost less than a snowmobile. You can be quite comfortable without standing headroom.

But he was right about the hot showers. It was a shower that got me looking for a bigger boat.

In spite of what the soap and deodorant commercials on TV would have you believe, it's not necessary to shower every day. You can bathe in a bucket. The bucket on 'Dreamer' gets plenty of use. Besides bailing the dinghy, it serves as a live bait well, emergency toilet, bath tub, and, with a little toilet plunger as an agitator, a washing machine. Seasick guests may barf in it. Remembering all those uses, I don't like to wash my hair in the bucket.

With towel, soap, and shampoo bottle in hand, I had walked the half mile from the visitor's dock to the marina showers. When I poured out some shampoo, it wasn't shampoo. There was lamp oil in my shampoo bottle.

By the time I had stomped back to the boat, I was steaming mad. "Ralph, what's this in my shampoo?"

"That's the lamp oil."

"What's it doing in a shampoo bottle?"

"The lamp oil bottle was too big." Ralph gave me an apologetic look and traded bottles. "This is your shampoo. I put a label on the lamp oil. I guess it came off. Sorry."

"Sorry won't dry my towel."

"Use mine."

The mix-up was his fault. To conserve space aboard 'Dreamer' Ralph got a square, plastic storage bin and tried to organize all the liquids: shampoo, conditioner, dish liquid and so on, all in smaller containers. About the only thing in its original packing is the formaldehyde to disinfect the portable toilet. Fortunately, Ralph can't transfer the aerosols pressure cans, or he'd mistake anti-mildew spray for shaving cream.

I stomped back to the showers swearing to teach him a lesson.

I agree that on a boat there has to be a place for everything and everything has to be put back. For instance, the binoculars always have to be put back in the same place so when you need them, there they are. You can't go berserk in a frantic search. The same applies to other instruments, like the hand bearing compass and the winch handles.

In the galley, the can opener has to be put back or it will disappear in the clutter. I swear, once I thought we would starve before we found that opener. It was put in a safe place so it wouldn't get lost, except we had forgotten where that safe place was. I finally put it on a string so it can't get away.

But lamp oil in a shampoo bottle? That had to be a booby trap.

At home Ralph has this thing about bottles. He harps about bottles in the bath tub. "What's this? Another shampoo?"

"That's conditioner, Ralph. Put it back."

At the grocery he buys the large, economy size to save money and then transfers stuff to smaller containers. Once he bought a whole gallon of soy sauce because it was a deal. There's nothing like setting the table for a Chinese meal complete with chop sticks and plunking down a gallon jug of soy sauce. It ruins the ambience. For years I've been struggling to transfer that soy sauce into little bottles.

Once I forgot and put soy sauce into a cake instead of vanilla extract. What was more infuriating, Ralph didn't notice.

When I got back to the boat I handed Ralph his wet towel and investigated the bottle bin. "What's this, Ralph?" I asked him, holding up a plastic bottle from cooking oil.

"That's stove alcohol. "

"The label's come off. How am I supposed to remember this?"

"Just smell it. "

"Lamp oil in this bottle. Stove alcohol in this one. What's the cooking oil in?"

"The detergent bottle."

I don't know what's worse, filling the kerosene lamp with detergent or making pancakes flambeau in lamp oil. Ralph's scheme for stowing all those liquids could be dangerous. "This is really stupid, Ralph. I'm glad you never got that charcoal grill. You'd probably have put starter fluid in a shampoo bottle. Lucky I don't smoke."

Our alcohol stove isn't good at frying steaks. Ralph thought about one of those charcoal grills that mounts on the rail, but I reminded him that smoke from a boat is a recognized distress signal. We wouldn't want the Coast Guard to intervene and put out our steaks. Even Heinz ketchup won't rescue a scorched steak smothered with dry powder bicarbonate of soda.

In our backpacking days Ralph and I had a little one burner gasoline stove he picked up in Germany during his military service. It was like a blow torch on end. The only fuel it required was ordinary gasoline, and we carried a small aluminum bottle that could last more than a week. There was no risk of confusing the aluminum gasoline bottle with the canteen of drinking water.

On 'Dreamer' we cook on an alcohol stove. Ralph would prefer kerosene. Kerosene doesn't blow up like gasoline but burns hotter than alcohol. It's also easier to find and costs a fraction of the price of alcohol. But a kerosene stove needs two kinds of fuel, not one. The stove has to be pre-warmed with alcohol so the tubes are hot enough to vaporize the fuel. A kerosene stove wouldn't reduce the number of fuels aboard. More little bottles with labels coming off.

Studying the contents of the bottle bin, I realized how many fuels and liquids we do have aboard. Of course, we never keep gasoline in the living space. The gasoline can stays in the vented lazaret, and there's a bulkhead to keep any fumes from getting into the cabin where the galley stove might ignite them.

I fired up the little alcohol stove and stowed the bin with those confusing bottles. Using the opener on its string,

I opened the chicken chow mein one can for the sauce, one for the veggies. So much for a two burner stove.

I now had two reasons for a bigger boat: a shower and a galley I could stand up in instead of twisting my back.

I would like an oven like we have in our pick-up camper. The camper stove uses LP gas. On a boat, LP gas bottles have to be stowed securely in a vented lazaret of their own. No little nuisances in Ralph's bottle bin.

'Dreamer' has no room for a gas bottle lazaret. Dreaming about a galley with a real oven, I set the table for dinner. Imagine, a gimbaled stove with an oven. We could have freshly baked bread instead of damp crackers or limp chow mein noodles.

A bigger boat would also have better places to stow things. Separate places. Cooking stuff in one cupboard. Cleaning stuff in another. Flammables in another. Everything in its place, not one jumble. No mix-ups. No transferring stuff to smaller containers. No shampoos with lamp oil.

Ralph stays in the cockpit while I'm cooking. There's not room in the cabin for two to move around at once. He didn't see the surprise I was arranging for him. He looked in through the hatch. "What's cookin'?"

"Chinese food out of a can."

"With green tea?"

"Sorry, this is only a two burner stove. I'm using   both pots for the chow mein."

"No problem. I see you're having a beer. I'll have   one, too." He lifted the floor board and fished a bottle of Moosehead out of the bilge.

I served up the dinner.

"Your health," Ralph said and lifted a Moosehead bottle. He nearly gagged. "What's this?"

"Soy sauce."

He gave me a suspicious look. "Soy sauce in a beer bottle?"

"Ralph, couldn't you tell by the smell? You're lucky it wasn't lamp oil."

"I wouldn't put lamp oil in a food container. Blech!"

"Oh, no? How about a shampoo bottle?"

Chapter 30

TERRITORIAL RIGHTS

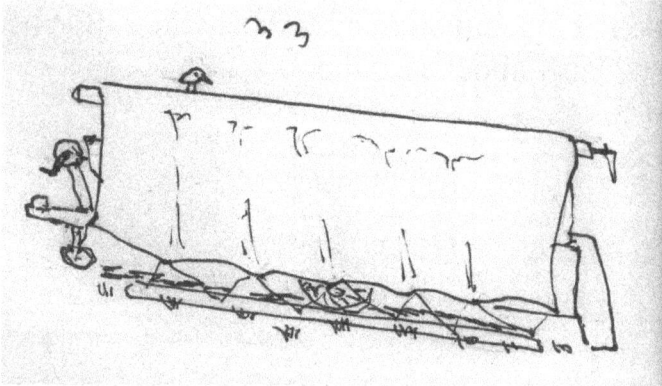

Our winter lay-up was complicated by squirrels. Squirrels may be cute, scampering around on the branches of our oak tree, but they are rodents and can be devilishly hard to get rid of. We sympathized with our neighbors, Ted and Gladys, when squirrels got into their attic. We laughed at Ted's antics at first, but it wasn't funny when Ted came out with a shot gun to blast one of those gray demons. It scampered onto the power line and-- you guessed it. Ted shot the wire.

The squirrel got away. But the police came, followed by the power company, in force, and Mr. Holzkopf of the "Keep our Neighborhood Neat Committee."

Holzkopf is the one who hates Ralph for parking our camper in the driveway, even though it's too high to get into the garage. He threatened us with banishment from the neighborhood when he thought we were going to store our boat in the front yard.

"It's only these older homes in the subdivision that have these problems."

"You mean the wrong kind of people?" Ralph suggested.

Holzkopf wasn't ready to admit that. "Power lines above ground."

"Think if the line was buried. Then we'd have a mole problem," Ralph said. "Imagine Ted blasting at moles. Think of the holes in the lawn."

Holzkopf sneered. "Ted won't discharge a firearm in the neighborhood again."

"What about dynamite? That'd get rid of both moles and crabgrass." Ralph was referring to the notorious weed ordinance and the battle with the lady who has an herb garden.

"Really, Quarterdeck. Some people don't understand the meaning of community."

"People aren't the problem. Squirrels are. You and your committee should draw up an ordinance against squirrels."

Ralph didn't know how right he was. The squirrels finally left Ted and Gladys, but they moved into our territory when we laid 'Dreamer' up for the winter. We didn't find out at first.

I enjoy watching those squirrels from the kitchen window as they play tag on the branches of the oak tree. Not being a grass fetishist, I don't mind them burying a few acorns in the lawn. A squirrel does have to lay something aside for the winter, just as we have to get the boat put away.

There's more to winter lay-up than hauling the boat on its trailer and backing it over the rose bushes into the back yard. We did it on a Sunday, planning to take everything out of the boat later. When we came back to finish the job we were in for a surprise.

You wouldn't believe how much stuff a boat contains. There's the life jackets, not just for us, but for whatever guests might come aboard. If left aboard all winter, the cushions may get damp and musty. There's the fire extinguishers, the radio and depth sounder, the battery, sails, boom cover, flags, awning, and anything else that might succumb to dampness and freezing. The stuff seems to expand like a self-inflating dingy in an elevator. The pile keeps growing until you wonder how you ever got that much stuff aboard a mere 23 footer. Ralph even has an old canoe paddle he keeps tucked away "in case of an emergency." That, at least, can stay aboard all winter, along with the anchors, fenders, and assorted coils of line.

The outboard motor has to come in, too, just in case there's a bit of water in the lower unit. Can't risk that freezing. Rather than let it spoil and turn to resins, the gas left in the tank goes into Ralph's truck. The bit of two cycle lubricating oil doesn't hurt. I won't have the gas can in the house. Too dangerous. If some spilled and evaporated it would take only the spark from a light switch to blow us all up.

The pile of boat gear scattered on the lawn around 'Dreamer' just grew and grew. Where were we going to put it all?

I remembered Doctor B--- the dentist and his pregnant wife who had been in our boating safety class. They live in a luxury condo down town and invited us to dinner the weekend we all graduated. Sitting in their posh dining room and wondering if Ralph and I would ever be able to afford a real dining room table, I noticed some gear in the corner. "What's that?" I asked.

"The boat radios," Dr. B--- had answered.

When I went to their guest bathroom later, I discovered an outboard motor beside the commode. The shower curtain was drawn. Behind it, stacked to the ceiling, were the sail bags from his 39 footer. I didn't realize how huge sail bags for a 39 footer could be. Their Zodiac inflatable boat stood at the side of their living room looking like a stuffed hippopotamus. I didn't inspect their closets.

I swore then that I wasn't going to have sail bags in our only bath tub or radios in the dining room. But where would we put it all? Here was Ralph, standing on his head in the lazaret, finding more stuff we didn't realize we had.

He shouted, "Nuts!"

"What's the matter, Ralph?"

He came up, red faced, like a diver out of breath, and showed me a handful. "Acorns. Those damned squirrels have commandeered our vessel for winter storage."

At that moment an acorn dropped onto the deck with a thump.

We looked up at the oak tree above us. The squirrel chattered and dropped another acorn.

"Bug off!" Ralph shouted, and threw the handful of acorns.

Swearing, Ralph removed a bucketful of acorns from the lazaret. After some puzzling he announced, "They got in through the ventilators."

A rat can come up through a toilet, or get through a hole the size of a quarter. A field mouse seeking winter shelter can wriggle through a hole the size of a dime. I had heard about people's boats being invaded by the occasional ship's rat, but didn't expect squirrels.

To keep the squirrels out, we had to remove the lazaret ventilators, put quarter inch galvanized hardware cloth over the holes, then reinstall them. It took some dexterity to reach way under the coaming and not drop the nuts and washers while Ralph tried to tighten the bolts.

We couldn't put hardware cloth over the cabin slide. The spaces the mosquitoes used as an expressway on hot summer nights were big enough to admit some winter rodent. The mushroom vent was safe. We had even put screen inside its cover to keep out mosquitoes. But there had to be ventilation or, come spring, we might find the boat black with mildew. I didn't want an electric heater aboard. There'd be the danger of fire and the power bill.

"Moth balls," Ralph said. "We'll leave moth balls in the boat."

"That works for skunks, but do squirrels care?"

"They might like them if they have moths in their fur. Maybe D-Con poison."

I didn't want to discover the dried corpse of some squirrel when we recommissioned in the spring, even that pesky squirrel in our oak tree.

First, we had to stow all that gear. We have a two car garage, and since the camper won't fit in one of the bays, and Holzkopf's vigilante committee won't permit outside parking, our aluminum fishing boat on its trailer is inside. We piled most of the stuff in the aluminum boat.

Not the sail bags. Ralph lugged them upstairs and up the folding ladder to the attic space. Standing on the ladder and surveying that unfinished space, he remembered Ted and Gladys. Squirrels had gotten into their attic.

I caught him stuffing newspapers in the sail bags. "What are you doing, Ralph?"

"Remember our boat hunting expeditions and the sails that were ruined when field mice nested in them? Just in case, I'm providing alternate nesting material."

"Wait until we've checked the sails thoroughly, Ralph. We want to make sure no threads are broken. Winter's a good time to make preventive repairs, like running a line of extra zigzag stitching to reinforce the seams of that old mainsail. And what about the slugs for the mast track?"

"Right. Gee, Irma, you think of everything."

For the time being, the sail bags were stacked in the bedroom by the sewing machine.

I changed the lower unit grease on the outboard motor and Ralph cleaned the spark plugs and sprayed some WD-40 inside the cylinders to prevent rust. Since the garage isn't heated, the outboard ended up standing behind the bar in the wreck room under that awful, plastic-bosomed female figurehead.

Winter lay-up took longer than we thought. There was a forgotten bottle of beer at the bottom of the bilge and some rusty bottle caps. And how did my old sun visor end up in the ice box? Under the galley stove I found the remains of Ralph's secret stash. "What's this, Ralph? Mouse heaven?"

"What do you mean?"

"Some of your old M&M chocolates. And a couple of graham crackers. Soggy graham crackers. Yuck."

I made Ralph dry out the bilge and pump the holding tank and the water box for the depth sounder. He added RV anti freeze to both tanks to eliminate any risk of freezing.

We made a list of all repairs that had to be done during the winter. I needed some new Velcro tape for the companionway screen. Sunlight had destroyed the fuzzy Nylon. One of the port holes, the one over my bunk that leaks, would have to be taken out and set in new bedding compound. The starboard block for the main sheet was worn out and needed replacing. Lots of little things.

Ralph got a box of mothballs and put them wherever he thought a squirrel might want to nest. There was nothing edible inside the boat. No crackers. No moldy chocolates.

Just in case, Ralph left a roll of paper towels on the cabin sole. "If we do get field mice," he said, "Better that they use this for nesting materials and not the curtains or carpeting."

The squirrel watched us from the oak tree when we put on the canvas tarp. Ralph shook a fist at him. "You better stay out," he said. The squirrel dropped another acorn.

"Missed!"

First, Ralph put braces under the mast on its carrier. A mast is meant to stand straight up, not to be loaded and bent out of shape by the weight of a tarp and winter snow.

All sharp corners had to be padded. We had seen carelessly-covered boats in some yards. Sharp corners invariably chafed canvas that flapped in the wind, if they didn't poke holes. I knew from our tenting days that ropes shouldn't be too tight, either, because rain would shrink the canvas and put too much strain on the grommets.

We still hadn't solved the squirrel problem. We didn't want to wrap the boat tightly. Ventilation was necessary, or dampness might not only cause mildew but warp the paneling inside. We needed to climb aboard from time to time to inspect or do those odd jobs before it got too cold. Even if we had wrapped the boat tightly, that wouldn't keep out the squirrels. They could just chew a hole in the canvas.

When 'Dreamer' was all buttoned up and no boat stuff remained in the back yard we had a sense of finality and sadness. There was a hint of frost in the air. The leaves had to be raked in time for the community mulcher to suck them up off the curb. We did a quick and dirty job of that, but the acorns were hard to get up.

"I have an idea," Ralph said. He climbed under the canvas and got a bucket out of the lazaret. In no time he had filled it with acorns.

Tail twitching nervously, the squirrel watched and scolded from a safe distance. Ralph held up the bucket of acorns and shouted up at his audience in the oak tree. "Look at this!"

The squirrel saw the bucket.

"These are for you," Ralph said. He made a show of putting the bucket under the boat trailer where it would stay dry. "Peace!"

That squirrel must be pretty proud, having somehow persuaded human servants to gather acorns and provide other foods. Whenever Ralph or I go out to work on the boat we put some tidbits under the trailer for the squirrel. I can watch him from the kitchen window. He sometimes runs across the canvas cover, but never goes inside.

We seem to have reached a territorial understanding.

Chapter 31

SOME FINAL WORDS

That about wraps it up for the sailing season. Mind you, we're still boating. Winter doesn't stop that. There's a path through the snow from the back door to 'Dreamer' under its cover. Ralph or I sneak out on some pretext or other. Last week we went over the sails, checking for loose threads, chafe, etc.

I brought in the log with its guest register and the record of our two radio contacts. Ralph says we should paste in photographs of some of the places we sailed to. "Make a scrapbook of it," he says, but the best pictures would be the ones that weren't taken. How do you take a photo of a freighter passing, invisible, in the fog? Or Ralph at midnight caught naked on deck in the rain, trying to stop a leak? Or the two of us terrified during that lightning storm?

Ralph says I should make some sketches, little drawings of what it was like. We have a talented friend, Peter Wells, who could do that. I'll make a note to ask him and stick it on the refrigerator.

Ralph bought the LORAN charts and a handbook on how to use it. We don't have GPS, but I can see it coming. With all those electrics on board that will mean he'll want a solar panel to keep the battery charged. I'll have to watch the budget!

That kid at the marina who couldn't understand why people would invest so much so they could spend their vacations cramped in tiny cabins obviously wasn't ready for boating. Ralph and I started out as back packers sleeping in a two person tent and cooking on a single burner camp stove. Compared to sleeping on rocks and getting dressed in the prone position, 'Dreamer's sitting headroom was luxury.

We graduated from a tent to our pickup camper with the aluminum fishing boat trailed behind. We got used to rambling around, looking for new places, seeing new sights, and exploring new waters. We like that concept called "self-contained." Independent.

We got tired of driving busy highways from one crowded campground to another. Those hundred thousand dollar motor homes towing Honda Civics don't strike us as roughing it. Plugging into the power pole so you can watch the same TV game show you saw at home isn't what I'd call getting away from the rat race. It's not our idea of camping. It strikes me that the only adventure to that would be the search for a parking place smaller than a ten acre shopping mall.

We haven't used the pick-up camper since we bought 'Dreamer.' We should probably sell it and the aluminum fishing boat, combine our resources and look for a bigger boat, one with space for a gimbaled stove with an oven and a wet locker, maybe even standing headroom in the head. Just a thought, you understand. A holding tank for the head would increase our range. A boat of around twenty-seven feet would do it. That's the typical size for cruising boats that sail beyond all horizons.

When I think of the annual depreciation and insurance on a hundred thousand dollar motor home, or the property tax and expense of a summer cabin on a lake echoing with the roar of water skiers, our little boat is cheap. A boat is a good investment. There are hundred year old boats still in service, and in spite of some blistering, fiberglass hulls seem to go on forever. There are so many used boats out there, a smart shopper who is patient can find a bargain.

And if you can live without shore power, a water hose, and daily hot showers, you don't have to pay to park a boat. The world's gotten too crowded with people, but you can still anchor someplace and not be disturbed. Just you, the water, the fish, and the birds. It's getting back to basics in a world that's gotten too complicated.

Ralph says he once heard a recording of the sound in the womb. The unborn baby is surrounded by liquid. The sea is the womb of all life. Lying in our bunks in the dark and listening to the sound of water against the hull is like being in the womb again. That's about as fundamental as you can get.

Waking up at dawn to the sound and sights of a new place gives you new perspectives. Birds, not bill boards. Fishing, crabbing, or clamming for our dinner gives us a feeling of self-reliance, like Robinson Crusoe or Swiss family Quarterdeck.

Sitting down here in the wreck room with that full-bosomed plastic ship's figurehead behind the bar, I realize how far Ralph and I have come since he first got the boating bug. We've learned more than we ever expected, imagined, or thought possible.

We've learned about navigation, tides, currents, electronics, physics, fabrics, fuels, wind and weather. We've learned how to take care of ourselves, to survive when things got nasty. We've learned to live in a new harmony with the elements. We've can identify some distant stars and planets and recognize water birds and marine life. Boating's been not only an adventure for the spirit, but a source of intellectual enlightenment. Like a college education, but more fun. Maybe one day we'll know enough to volunteer to teach one of those Coast Guard Auxiliary courses.

We've also gotten to know each other better. When you both have jobs, as we do, a marriage can fall into routine, something habitual that happens briefly between chores. If being aboard 'Dreamer' reminded us of our camping honeymoon, it's partly because, on the boat, we're together in close proximity twenty-four hours a day.

Sure, we tease each other like a couple of kids, but we're having fun.

Ralph says I'm being sentimental. Me? Irma Quarterdeck? Look at him, sitting there feeling "salty" in his silly Moosehead beer tee shirt and Greek fisherman's hat. He says he wants me to study the new chart and make plans for our next cruise, but I know him. He wants me close enough to hug. As Christopher Robin would say of his friend, Winnie the Pooh, "Silly old bear."

Yours faithfully,

Irma Quarterdeck
Irma Quarterdeck

Harley L. Sachs

Author's note

The sea shanties included here are selected from the 1910 edition of *Ships, Sea Songs and Shanties* collected by W. B. Whall and published by James Brown and Son in Glasgow, Scotland. His collection of previously published shanties was published before the copyright laws were enacted and are in the public domain. Feel free to copy these as you wish.

Ralph's Sea Shanty collection

Harley L. Sachs

The original title page

SHIPS,

SEA SONGS and SHANTIES

Collected by

W. B. WHALL, Master Mariner.

The Songs harmonised by R. H. WHALL, Mus.Bac., F.R.C.O., Etc.

Illustrations by VERONICA WHALL

GLASGOW :

JAMES BROWN & SON, 52-56 DARNLEY STREET, POLLOKSHIELDS

1910

· Preface. ·

THESE Songs have appeared in the *Nautical Magazine* and *Yachting Monthly*. By the courtesy of the Editors I now publish them in book form. A few portraits of celebrated sailing-ships of the date in which these songs were sung are added. I set myself a plain task, namely, to write down these songs, music and words, as I heard them sung at sea by sailors. I have, therefore, not searched through the British Museum for the correct (?) wording or tune in any case. As to the spelling of "shanty" I see no reason why, because shore people have fancied a derivation of the word and written it "chanty," I should follow. It was not so pronounced at sea, and to spell it so is misleading. I have good reasons for supposing that the presumed French derivation of this word is wrong.

The book would be shorn of half its value were it not for the harmonising of the Songs by my brother, R. H. Whall, Mus. Bac., and the clever Drawings of my niece, Miss Veronica Whall.

I hope this attempt to rescue these old Songs from oblivion will find favour.

W. B. WHALL.

1910.

Harley L. Sachs

A-Roving.

THE motive of this favourite sea song is very old indeed, and appears (in slightly varying forms in many writings, *e.g.*, in Thomas Heywood's *Rape of Lucrece.*

In Am-ster-dam there liv'd a maid—Mark well what I do say.

In Am-ster-dam there liv'd a maid, And she was mis-tress of her trade.

I'll go no more a - rov - ing with you fair maids.

CHORUS.

A - rov - ing, a - rov - ing, Since rov-ing's been my ru - in,

I'll go no more a - rov - ing with you fair maids.

> I put my arm around her waist—
>   Mark well what I do say.
> I put my arm around her waist,
>   Says she, "Young man, you're in great haste!"
> I'll go no more a-roving with you fair maids.
>
>   (*Chorus*).—A-roving, a-roving,
>   Since roving's been my ruin,
>   I'll go no more a-roving with you fair maids.
>   Etc., etc.

Harley L. Sachs

Blow the Man Down.

THIS comes from the old Atlantic sailing packet ships. "Blow" in those days was equivalen
to "knock." The third mate in those ships was endearingly termed the third "blowe
and striker," the second mate being the "greaser."

O blow the man down, bul-lies, blow the man down !

Way - ay, blow the man down. O blow the man down in

Liv - er - pool town! Give me some time to blow the man down.

As I was a-walking down Paradise Street,
A saucy young p'liceman I happened to meet.

Says he, "You're a Black Baller by the cut of your hair,
I know you're a Black Baller by the clothes that you wear.

"You've sailed in a packet that flies the Black Ball,
You've robbed some poor Dutchman of boots, clothes and all."

"O p'liceman, O p'liceman, you do me great wrong,
I'm a 'Flying Fish sailor' just home from Hong Kong."

They gave me three months in Walton Jail
For booting and kicking and blowing him down.

There was another set of words to this shanty, which went as follows :—

Come all you young fellows that follow the sea,
Now pray pay attention and listen to me.

'Twas aboard a Black Baller I first served my time,
And in that Black Baller I wasted my prime.

214

Harley L. Sachs

Blow, Ye Winds, in the Morning.

THIS was a song of the midshipman's berth rather than the forecastle, as was also the song t follows on page 36, "Boston."

As I walked out one sun-ny morn to view the meadows round, I

spied a pret-ty prim-rose lass come tripping o'er the ground, Sing-ing

Blow, ye winds, in the morn - ing, Blow, ye winds, Hi! Ho!

Harley L. Sachs

Brush a-way the morn-ing dew, Blow, ye winds, Hi! Ho!

I saddled me an Arab steed and saddled her another,
And off we rode together just like sister and like brother.

We rode along until we came to a field of new-mown hay,
Says she, "Young man, this is the place for men and maids to play."

I took her from her Arab steed and gently laid her down,
Says she, "Young man, oh pray take care, you'll spoil my new silk gown."

Etc., etc.

Harley L. Sachs

Bound for the Rio Grande.

Now, you Bowery ladies, we'd have you to know,
    O, you Rio!
We're bound to the Southward, O Lord, let us go!
        For I'm bound to the Rio Grande.
                (*Chorus as before*).

So it's pack up your donkey and get under way,
The girls we are leaving can take our half-pay.

We'll sell our salt cod for molasses and rum,
And get back again 'fore Thanksgiving has come.

And good-bye, fare-you-well, all you ladies of town,
We've left you enough for to buy a silk gown.

Thanksgiving Day answers in America to our Christmas.

Harley L. Sachs

Can't you Dance the Polka.

As I walk'd down the Broadway, one ev·'ning in Ju - ly,

I met a maid who axed my trade, "A sail - or John." says I;

And a - way you san - tee, my dear An - nie.

O you New York girls, can't you dance the pol - ka?

To Tiffany's I took her,
  I did not mind expense ;
I bought her two gold earings,
  They cost me fifty cents.
    Chorus—And a-way, etc.

Says she, "You lime-juice sailor,
  Now see me home you may."
But when we reached her cottage-door
  She unto me did say—
    Chorus—And a-way, etc.

"My flash man he's a Yankee,
  With his hair cut short behind ;
He wears a tarry jumper,
  And he sails in the Black Ball Line."
    Chorus—And a-way, etc.

Harley L. Sachs

Doo me Ama.

THIS is a good example of a class of song peculiarly the sailor's own, which treated of Jack's successful amours and in which "maid servants follow him all the world over in what women are often apt to prefer to petticoats (*videlicet*, trousers). 'Mistress's only daughters' pine and die for him. Ladies single him out as an object of devoted attachment. And even princesses deign to bestow their love upon a humble son of Neptune."

As Jack was walk-ing thro' the square, He met a la-dy and a squire. Now Jack he heard the squire say, To-night with you I mean to stay. Doo-me a-ma, Din-ghy a-ma, Doo-me a-ma day.

"I will tie a string to my little finger,
And the other end hang out of the window,
    Then you must come and pull the string,
    I'll come down and let you in."
        Doo me ama, etc.

"Damn my eyes," says Jack, "if I do not venture
For to pull the string hanging out of the window."
    So Jack he went and pulled the string,
    She came down and let him in.
        Doo me ama, etc.

"Oh, what is that which smells so tarry?
I've nothing in the house that's tarry;
    It's a tarry sailor down below,
    Kick him out—in the snow."
        Doo me ama, etc.

"Oh, what d'you want, you tarry sailor?
You've come to rob me of my treasure!"
    "Oh no," says Jack, "I pulled the string,
    You came down and let me in."
        Doo me ama, etc.

Harley L. Sachs

Farewell and Adieu.

Fare - well and a - dieu un - to you, Span - ish la - dies,
Chorus—We'll rant and we'll roar like true Bri - tish sai - lors,

Fare - well and a - dieu to you, la - dies of Spain;
We'll rant and we'll roar a - cross the salt seas,

For it's we've re - ceived or - ders for to sail for old Eng - a - lund,
Un til we strike sound - ings in the chan - nel of old Eng - a - land.

D C. for Chorus.

But we hope ve - ry soon we shall see you a - gain.
From Ush - ant to Scil - ly is thir - ty - five leagues.

Then we hove our ship to with the wind at sou'west, my boys,
We hove our ship to our soundings for to see ;
 So we rounded and sounded,
 And got forty-five fathoms,
We squar-ed our main yard, up channel steered we.

Now the first land we made it is call-ed the Deadman,
Then Ram Head off Plymouth, Start, Portland, and Wight ;
 We sail-ed by Beachy,
 By Fairlee and Dungeness,
Until we came abreast of the South Foreland Light.

24

221

Harley L. Sachs

Homeward Bound.

IN sailing-ship days this song was a prime favourite and was sung all the world over. In American ships you might hear it begun with :—

> " To Pensacola town I'll bid adieu,
> To my lovely Kate and Pretty Sue."

Sunderland " Jamie " would sing—

> " At the Sunderland docks I'll bid adieu,"

and so on round all our sea ports.

The version here given is the London one. The " Dog and Bell " is probably legendary, for it appears in most versions; but whereas the American sang of " Mother Langley," the Londoner sang of " Old Grouse," a celebrity unknown to me ; possibly he, too, was legendary, for " grouse " (to growl) was a common sea word in those days, as it still is in the army. Malabar is evidently chosen for the sake of the rhyme ; any foreign port would have done as well.

At the Blackwall docks we bid a-dieu to love-ly Kate and pret-ty Sue; Our anchor's weigh'd and our sails unfurl'd, And we're bound to plow the

wat'ry world, And say we're out-ward bound, Hur-rah we're outward bound.

The wind it blows from the East-North-East,
Our ship she sails nine knots at least,
Our roaring guns we'll well supply,
And while we have powder never say die.
　　And say we're outward bound, etc.

And when we get to Malabar,
Or some other port not quite so far,
Our captain will our wants supply,
And while we've grub we'll never say die.
　　And say we're outward bound, etc.

Then at last our captain comes on board,
Our sails are bent, we're manned and stored,
The Peter's hoisted at the fore,
Good-bye to the girls we'll see no more.
　　For we are homeward bound, etc.

One day the man on the look-out,
Proclaims a sail with a joyful shout.
Can you make her out? I think I can,
She's a pilot standing out from the land.
　　Hurrah, we're homeward bound, etc.

Now when we get to the Blackwall Docks,
The pretty young girls come down in flocks;
One to the other you'll hear them say,
" O, here comes Jack with his ten months' pay."
　　For I see you're homeward bound, etc.

223

Harley L. Sachs

Stormalong.

A VERY favourite old shanty and full of character, particularly in the tune. The usual words are given here; seldom was any attempt made at improvisation.

O Storm-y, he is dead and gone: To my way you storm a - long.

O Storm y was a good old man; Ay, ay, ay, Mis-ter Storm-a - long.

We'll dig his grave with a silver spade,
And lower him down with a golden chain.

I wish I was old Stormy's son,
I'd build a ship of a thousand ton.

I'd fill her with New England rum,
And all my shell-backs they'd have some.

O Stormy's dead and gone to rest,
Of all the sailors he was best.

About Harley L. Sachs:

Harley L. Sachs is the author of many novels, short stories, magazine articles and newspaper columns. His short stories have been broadcast on the BBC World Service short wave and on Oregon Public Radio's Golden Hours. His awards for writing are too numerous to list.

Harley and his wife Ulla live in Portland, Oregon.

Harley L. Sachs

If you enjoyed *Ahoy! Quarterdeck,* you may like *Hunting the Mail Buoy and other Hazards to Navigation* a book of nautical cartoons by the author. Here's a sample:

THE SOVIET SUBMARINE CAPTAIN'S DISGUISE WAS OK UNTIL SOMEONE MAILED A DEAD FISH DOWN HIS SNORKEL

I DON'T CARE IF IT IS FROM ADMIRAL PERRY. IF IT AIN'T GOT A STAMP, IT DON'T GET DELIVERED!

Here's a list of books by Harley L. Sachs:

MYSTERY NOVELS

The Mystery Club Series

THE MYSTERY CLUB SOLVES A MURDER

First and most popular of the Mystery Club series. Mary Higgins finds the body of Dora Reed on the roof of the Plaza retirement building, notifies the police, then tells the Mystery Club. They assume several suspects: the manager of the Plaza, Dora's son Donald, or a Plaza employee. Dora's husband, Ed Sutherland, is in Hawaii on board the yacht Miss Chief with an all girl crew. Carrying on their own investigation, the Mystery Club finally suspects Sutherland, though he seems to have a perfect alibi. If they can prove it to their satisfaction, will a court ever convict him-- if he can be found somewhere in the Pacific?

THE MYSTERY CLUB AND THE DEAD DOCTOR

Second in the Mystery Club series. The Mystery Club consists of five elderly women who live at the Rose Plaza and discuss mysteries written by women. The Mystery Club ladies have no idea of the consequences when Viola Cartwright, their blind member, asks them to go over her Medicare bills. That leads to suspicion about the identity of her personal assistant, Dorothy Anderson, who turns out to be using a stolen identity. Viola's doctor runs a phony clinic owned by a member of the Russian Mafia. Soon the investigation of Medicare bills leads to murder and tragedy, stopped only by the courage of Mary Higgins.

THE MYSTERY CLUB AND THE HIDDEN WITNESS

Third in the Mystery Club series. The ladies of the Mystery Club discover one of the residents is a crook under WITSEC, the witness protection program. He apparently keeps dipping into the employee gift fund. The Mystery Club bands together to track down the missing money, but what they discover is danger.

THE MYSTERY CLUB AND THE SERIAL WIDOW

Fourth in the Mystery Club series. Caroline Kostinsky, new resident at the Rose Plaza, is a widow four times over and she's looking for a fifth husband in retired General Hardcastle, but when drunk she says she killed all of her husbands. Except for her confession, there's no evidence. Now what?

DELIVER ME FROM EVIL

Responding to a posted invitation for new members for the Mystery Club, Judge Ira Kahane and Ursula Besette show up. Ursula, at a turning point in her life as a new Rose Plaza resident, is interested in Wicca and Kabala. Roberta Nelson believes one should not suffer a witch to live. Judge Kahane tries to lead Ursula on the right path, but there is conflict and tragedy coming.

WHITE SLAVE

Sequel to *The Mystery Club Solves a Murder.* The appearance of Ed Sutherland's gold bracelet in a Portland pawn shop revives retired detective Casey's interest in the cold case. He doesn't know that Sutherland has been picked up and is a slave on a Korean fishing boat. Sutherland, penniless, .without clothes or identification, is stranded in New Zealand. Can he find his way back to Portland and be somehow redeemed or face a death sentence for first degree murder?

The Irwin Glass Series

BETRAYAL

Prequel to *Retribution.* Irwin Glass, BA in Russian, MA in International Relations, has a promising career in the Foreign Service in Moscow until he is snared in a classic "honey pot" seduction. He's young and naïve, honest, always wants to do the right thing, but at every turn he is betrayed. The incident in Moscow destroys his career. He is accused of being a paid Soviet agent and is pursued by the consequences of his encounter with the KGB twenty years later. Some enemies never let go

RETRIBUTION

Sequel to *Betrayal.* Newly married to Ivy Hartshorn, Irwin Glass gets a dunning letter from the IRS for taxes on interest at the Washington, DC account he didn't think he had. It's a joint account with his missing birth daughter and the balance is huge. Assuming it's money Katya's KGB father of record, Vladimir Putinsky (now Putin) deposited for her living expenses, Irwin moves it to force her to contact him. But Ivy warns him that he is laundering money and the people it belongs to will come after him. Irwin's complicated life is catching up with him, but this time he will find retribution.

BURNT OUT

Irwin Glass is approached by FBI Agent Wilkins who asks for Irwin's lists of foreign students. Not satisfied he wants more and is looking for potential terrorists among the Moslem students. Gradually Irwin is sucked into the role of FBI informant on the Michigan Institute of Technology's Muslim Students' Association and the results are tragic.

THE IRWIN GLASS TRILOGY

All three Irwin Glass books in one package deal. The Irwin Glass Trilogy combines all three of the Irwin Glass Mysteries: "Betrayal," "Retribution," and "Burnt Out," following the chaotic career of Irwin Glass who began, in "Betrayal," as a state department clerk in Moscow only to be caught in a classic honey pot seduction. Betrayed at every turn, he was sent back to the United States in disgrace to try to start a new life. No such luck. His teaching career is upturned by the revelation that the Moscow seduction had a consequence in the form of a beautiful student Katya who claims to be his daughter. In "Retribution," Irwin's KGB nemesis is in the United States seeking political asylum, but in fact is fleeing the Russian Mafia with Irwin as quarry. After "Retribution," Irwin thinks he is home free of all that intrigue, but the local FBI agent has a hold on him and wants information about potential terrorists among Irwin's students at Michigan Institute of Technology. There are risks to being a reluctant FBI informant, and Irwin's reports may be misconstrued with tragic results. What Irwin and his wife really want is a normal life, but his mysterious Russian birth daughter Katya remains an enigma. Is she or isn't she?

Other Mysteries

MURDER BY MAIL

German exchange student Klaus Hitz is more interested in making money than in asking questions about his work assignment. He doesn't know that the industrialist father of his punk girl friend is using him in a terrorist conspiracy to kill everyone in the United States with a mass mailing of a scratch and sniff virus. The plot begins to unravel when a Polish nurse brings blood samples from Libya and alerts a CIA agent. While the CIA and FBI track down the terrorists, Klaus Hitz gradually figures it out. How can he avoid being murdered or imprisoned for being naive?

MURDER IN THE KEWEENAW

CIA agent recovering from Post traumatic Stress after failed missions in Finland and a divorce is fishing in Lake Superior when he snags a corpse. He thinks he has seen the girl before and his attempt to identify her leads him to a ring of deadly pornographers. It almost costs him his own life.

CONSPIRACY!

Technical writer Tom Godot can't believe his luck when CONSPIRACY!, the book he has co-written with the elusive Harold Stevenson, is a hit. The book details a plot to hijack communication satellites. As Tom crosses the country on his book tour, he is disturbed by people interested in early drafts and dogged by an NSA agent. Communicating by fax with his editor and by encrypted e-mail with the mysterious Stevenson, Tom reaches out in his loneliness to his California girl friend Sylvia Hanson who turns out to be a pivotal figure. There is another conspiracy, and Tom is part of it

THE GOLD CHROMOSOME

When Adam Rottman's childless Aunt Sadie Gold died, the eight cousins learned her estate was in an irrevocable trust, the proceeds going to Adam's sister Sarah while she lives. After Sarah's death, the money would go to the last surviving cousin. It's a fatal tontine Adam's lawyer brother Harold set up. Would the cousins kill each other for one million dollars? Sarah's car is found in the river, but not Sarah. That begins a series of mysterious deaths. Coincidence? Or

Murder? Who will be next? Adam and his psychologist wife Deborah must stop the chain before he, too, is eliminated.

BEN ZAKKAI'S COFFIN
Born of a Jewish father and a Catholic mother, Herman Bachrach insists he has no religion, but he is drawn by circumstance into a holocaust vendetta over gold stolen by a Swiss bank from Jewish depositors. Seduced by a woman who calls herself Diana, no last name, Herman is suspected by detective Sheehan to be her murderer. Someone else wants him dead.   His Jewish boss provides him with a lawyer, but sends him to Switzerland to finish the job "Diana" started. It's an assignment he can't refuse.   The result is an epiphany of identity that changes Herman's life forever.

THE LOLLIPOP MURDER
A warning for wannabe novelists! What happens when a stable of neurotic novelists who live in their pseudonyms and are bound by iron clad contracts are invited aboard their miserly Florida publisher's yacht for the Miami Book Fair only to find that they have no hope of ever earning a dime of royalties for their books? All this as Hurricane Gerta threatens to sink the yacht at the dock.   It's grounds for murder

NOVELS

SAM IN LOVE
A coming of age romance for mature young adults. U.S. Army life in Europe in the 1950's was an equivalent of the Grand Tour of the eighteenth century when young men traveled and sowed wild oats. Marty, roommate of Sam Logan, a PFC draftee serving in the US Army in Munich, Germany, says all Sam needs is to get laid. Sam is not a virgin, but has a Midwestern ethic and believes in love. He doesn't know quite what that is. No Casanova, Sam, through a series of tentative encounters, thinks he's found the love of his life.

STOPRAPE.COM
Kerstin Mikkola, a young TV reporter at KDUP in Marquette, Michigan has hopes of a better network job. Her interview with a marine victim or rape might be just the ticket. Her interview about the

web site StopRape.com goes viral on U-tube and Kerstin finds herself in the thick of consequences she did not anticipate.

THE ACCIDENTAL COURIER
A romance, road trip, and mystery all in one. Charles Kosko, retired orchard owner from Oregon, decides to take a bus trip in Europe and finds himself involved in a whistle-blower's scheme to discredit an American cell phone company that uses rare earths mined by slaves in the Congo. Unable to speak any foreign language, and without his US passport, he is picked up by a beautiful Israeli woman who says she is his driver. But is he really her prisoner? They are pursued by an African mining engineer, who hopes to intercept the delivery of stolen rare earths,

SCI-FI AND FANTASY

NEVER TRUST A TALKING HORSE
The narrator of this dystopian novel escapes preventive detention into a world he discovers has gone mad. Hungry, he is told he can eat for free at Lachumba's supper club, only to discover that he might be the main dish. He rescues Iris I. Iris from the ovens and in a series of episodes explores the insane world in search of a livelihood. He gradually realizes why he was incarcerated in the first place, but by then it is too late. His and Iris's roles have been reversed. Arrested, they are given a sadistic sentence which is their final challenge.

THE SEARCH FOR JESSE BRAM
Jesse Bram, the young hero of this metaphysical science fiction adventure, is unaware of his Jewish roots. An Eldre of mixed breed, he is marooned on the post apocalyptic shunned planet URth where technology and books have been destroyed. The URthlings variously view Jesse as a bringer of cargo for the half-breed prefect Hrod, as the reborn Savior by crypto-Christians, and as a link to the past by a remnant of Jews. The Galactic Federation suspects him of treason and he is pursued by an enigmatic Trinian policeman. If Jesse survives, will he be convicted? If acquitted, what next?

SHORT STORIES

THREADS OF THE COVENANT: THE JEWS OF RED JACKET

A collection of twenty-one short stories about Jewish life in small town America centering about two main characters, David Katz, the only Jewish boy in Red Jacket, and Richard Goldman, the only Jewish professor at Copper country Community College. Each story depicts another aspect of what it means to be a Jew in a small town as each character comes to realize his own identity.

MISPLACED PERSONS

Though set in different locales what these stories have in common is a central character who is out of his element, in the wrong place, coming to grips with cultural, generational, or physical displacement. In PROBLEM FOR THE TEACHER an expatriate fumbles for a living; in LIMBO an ex-G.I. is adrift in Copenhagen; in TRIUMPH OF THE WILL a nervous wreck seeks recuperation; in MISCALCULATION a would be tax evader succumbs to his own fears; in THE LIE a drunk gets himself into difficulties, and in THE GIRLS OF FREDERIKSHAVN an old man is trapped by girls looking for action.

YOOPER TALES AND OTHER FUNNY STUFF

Extracted from the massive volume of Sachs's published Essays and Columns: 1992-2011, this collection of stories related to Michigan's Upper Peninsula, known as the UP, home of Yoopers, reveals the truth about snow fleas, ice worms, the humungous fungus (world's largest living thing) and the rigors of winters in the remote north woods. You can also learn how to catch and cook the Mosquito Giganticus and why visitors won't come. Sachs has several awards for his humor.

AHOY! QUARTERDECK!

Originally published as IRMA QUARTERDECK REPORTS but re-released with new illustrations and, in the paperback edition, with sea shanties, this funny book is a series of boating anecdotes about Irma and her bumbling husband Ralph ("I can't believe I lost the anchor") Quarterdeck in their many boating adventures and mishaps. One reviewer says the book is as informative as Chapman's famous manual, but more fun. Readers will find plenty of laughs in this book and at the same time learn a great deal of boating fundamentals.

ANNA-LENA'S TROLL AND OHER STORIES
Each of the three Sachs daughters has a story in this children's book. "Anna-Lena's Troll" explores the nature of trolls, which represent the dark side of human behavior as Anna-Lena's nasty letter to Santa is rewarded by the gift of a nasty troll. "The Return of Baby Suzy" is the true story of Cynthia's worn out doll and its resurrection. "The Stars for Christmas" is the remarkable surprise Belinda got along with her new eye glasses. Other family stories are Christmas related.

NON-FICTION

THE MISADVENTURES OF CPL. SACHS
Adrift through college at Indiana University, author Sachs was drafted at the end of the Korean War. Physically unfit for combat, he was sent to Queer Company for basic training, then by a fluke was shipped out to Germany instead of Korea. Thus began his own version of the traditional Grand Tour.

FREELANCE NONFICTION ARTICLES
This third edition of a monograph on freelance writing first published by the Society for Technical Communication is newly updated. This little manual provides tips for interviewing, article structure, article preparation and submission, photography, and business practice.

CHILLY-CHILLY-BANG—HOW WE FREELANCED THROUGH EUROPE'S COLDEST WINTER IN A VW WITH A KID
Companion piece to *Freelance Nonfiction Articles*. The former is a how to book. This is a "how we did it" memoir. The author knew nothing about Volkswagens when they set off, but as they worked from VW dealer to dealer getting the old Combi fixed, he learned! It's as much a book for VW enthusiasts as it is for writers.

Both FREELANCE NONFICTION ARTICLES and *Chilly-Chilly-BANG! How we Freelanced Through Europe's Coldest Winter in a VW with a Kid* are combined in a double volume, *The Writing Life*.

THE 1957 SACHS ARCTIC EXPEDITION

After military service in Germany the author took the GI Bill to Sweden. With no income in the summer, and not even sure there was a road to the far north, he set off hitchhiking to North Cape, the northernmost point in Europe in search of the midnight sun. Illustrated.

FROM TENT TO CASTLE: MEMOIR OF A YEAR LONG HONEYMOON

Setting off from Stockholm, Sweden on rebuilt one speed bicycles, Harley and Ulla embarked on an open-ended honeymoon with no fixed destination and equipped with a tent, a thin double sleeping bag, a tiny gasoline stove, and $3000. After arriving in Britain, Ulla discovered she was pregnant. Tired of unrelenting rain, they advertised for a cheap place to spend the winter. They were offered the gatehouse to Borthwick Castle outside Edinburgh, Scotland for $25 a month by British author Theo Lang.

"IS"

As Bill Clinton said, "It all depends on what the meaning of "is" is."
A problem we all have is distinguishing between what is real and what is not.   This is in fact an age-old question.   This volume switches between classical instances of the problem to the author and his psychiatrist and his wife.   What is real? That all depends on the meaning of "real."

QUEER COMPANY

Not a gay novel, this is a fictionalized memoir of an experimental basic training unit at the end of the Korean War.   All the draftees were physically unfit for combat but the army didn't want to discharge them. Instead they got modified training in a company unfortunately designated Q.   In the Army phonetic alphabet Q is Queen, but Q company was called queer.   A copy is in the US Army historical archives.

Harley L. Sachs